THE CHURCH OF

BLUE COLUMNS

St Olave's Church, Mitcham, 1946

THE CHURCH OF BLUE COLUMNS

ANGLO-CATHOLICISM IN A NEW DISTRICT

St Olave, Mitcham, 1928–1939

by

Keith Penny

Published by St Olave's Mitcham PCC

St Olave's Church
Church Walk
London SW16 5JH
United Kingdom

©2013 St Olave's Mitcham PCC

ISBN 978-0-9926523-0-2

Printed by:

Book Printing UK
Remus House
Coltsfoot Drive
Peterborough
Cambridgeshire
PE2 9BF

With gratitude for two friendships:

Roy Brenchley, Priest, 1932–2010

Bernard Carnell, 1946–2005

PREFACE

During the first fifteen years of my residence in the parish of St Olave, Mitcham, I only rarely entered my parish church, my churchgoing loyalties then being elsewhere. When first I did so, during the later hours of the Passion Watch, I was dimly aware of blue columns and distant spaces; it was a building quite unlike the others in which I had worshipped. Through later events that I now see as providential I joined the congregation and then became a churchwarden. In 2000–1 the late Roy Brenchley asked me to provide a local history contribution to the parish profile that he was preparing as part of his training for ordination, and so I took my first look at the archives available in Morden Library, especially the typescript of Eric Montague's work on Longthornton. Soon afterwards I read Kenneth Richardson's book on the Twenty-five churches of Southwark, and the history by Ray Ninnis of the church building and its predecessor in Southwark that was published by Merton Historical Society. Eventually I began in 2008 the parish history presented here.

The building as it is today is easily viewed on the church's website at www.st-olaves.com, though the columns of the book's title are no longer blue. Alongside a narrative of the church's foundation and construction, I have analysed the finances of the parish; I have examined the life and character of the first Vicar in some detail, because he was clearly a remarkable man; and I have attempted a profile of the worshipping congregation in the years that led to World War Two. In particular I have described the kind of Anglican worship and practice that Fr Reginald Haslam worked to establish in a parish where there were no previous customs and where the worshippers came from different church backgrounds or from no background at all. Because the first services took place at Christmas 1927, at the same time as the rejection by Parliament, amid much anti-Catholic rhetoric, of the proposed revised Prayer Book, I have also looked at the religious opinions that the ordinary residents of Long Thornton might have found in the mass-market daily newspapers and asked whether national publicity about Protestants and Anglo-Catholics made any difference to Fr Haslam's establishment of Anglo-Catholic worship as the norm for St Olave's.

I have provided some explanations for those not familiar with Anglican and Anglo-Catholic language, as well as some background church history; I apologise if I have patronised some and stated the obvious to others.

ACKNOWLEDGEMENTS

A substantial contribution to the production costs of this book was made by the Anglo-Catholic History Society.

Much of the research was funded through the London Borough of Merton's provision of my Freedom Pass for travel around the capital.

I am particularly grateful to the staff of the following libraries and archives, and to those bodies that fund them: Barbican Music Library, London; British Library Newspapers, London; Cadbury Research Library, Birmingham; CCB Library, Westminster; Church of England Record Centre; Croydon Central Library; Guildhall Library, London; King's College, London, Archives; Kingston upon Thames Archives and Local History Service; Lambeth Archives; Lambeth Palace Library; London Metropolitan Archives; Merton Heritage & Local Studies Centre; Royal Institute of British Architects; Royal Military Academy, Sandhurst; Southwark Local History Library; Surrey History Centre, Woking; Sutton Local Studies Collection; The National Archives; Wandsworth Heritage Service; York Minster Library.

Individuals have contributed in several ways: Professor John Hines of Cardiff University wrote to me about Olaf; Gaynor Taylor read the text to see if it made overall sense; John Webb advised on the many details of typography that I had overlooked; Hugh Proctor helped with matters numerical; Fr Paul Ensor, Vicar of St Olave's Church 1995–2013, provided introductory letters; Paul Sharrock read the sections on architecture and A. C. Martin and allowed his reports on the church to be quoted; Valerie Bryant of Redbridge Information & Heritage found the picture of the organ at Monkhams; John W. Brown of the Streatham Society provided material from his collection of newspaper cuttings.

Canon John Gunstone consented to my using his rainbow categorisation of Anglo-Catholic practices; the Biographical Librarian of St John's College, Cambridge, kindly agreed to the use of material about Fr Haslam's time at Cambridge.

The following have given permission to reproduce pictorial material:

Lambeth Archives Department: Illustration 1
Merton Library & Heritage Service: Illustration 11
City of London, London Metropolitan Archives: Illustration 16
Southwark Local History Library: Illustration 15
Surrey History Centre: Illustrations 4, 5, 7, 10, 13
Trustees of the Lambeth Palace Library: front cover

CONTENTS

ILLUSTRATIONS

Front cover: Perspective drawing by A. C. Martin, 1930
Back cover: Advertisement for Building Fund, 1928
Frontispiece: From Parish Magazine, 1950
Title page: From Parish Magazine, 1952

Plates in the middle of the book:

Illustrations not credited in the text or in the acknowledgments have been copied from material held at St Olave's Church.

PRELIMINARIES

ANGLO-CATHOLIC, HIGH AND LOW

Though often used in this book, these are slippery terms, because many practices and furnishings once seen as Anglo-Catholic or High are now commonplace in Anglican churches, though often without the doctrines that justified them. Chapter 14 offers more explanation, if not more clarity.

OLAF, OLAVE AND TOOLEY

Though the church can be called "Saint Olave's", with a long "o" and a short "a", "St Olave's" is, or at least has been, in London (and York) pronunciation "St Olive's". My father used it in connection with the church in Hart Street, and two of the almsdishes from St Olave, Southwark, are engraved "St: Ollives. Ch. 1718". The saint, though, is usually "Saint Olaf", to discourage the supposition that Olave=Olive=female. Tooley Street in Southwark is a corruption over centuries of the church name, from "St Oley". A newspaper in 1737 referred to "St. Olave's Church, Southwark, (vulgarly call'd Tooly's)".

MITCHAM OR NORBURY?

St Olave's was, briefly, St Olave, Norbury, rather than St Olave, Mitcham. This is a demonstration of the uncertainty of location of the present Longthornton Ward of Merton, as well as of the parish. When asked "Where do you live?" I find it hard to give a simple answer. The postal district is London SW16, but two minutes' walk finds you in Croydon (CR) district. For a modern map, search "SW16 5JH" at www.achurchnearyou.com.

LONGTHORNTON OR LONG THORNTON?

"Long Thornton" was the form used during the period of this history.

COUNCILS

The local authority was Mitcham Urban District Council [from 1934 Mitcham Borough Council]. Surrey County Council retained responsibility for the building of schools.

"The Church's task is to preach not what is popular,

but what is true."

Fr Reginald Haslam, March 1932

1: LONESOME AND LONG THORNTON

Remembered in 1936, Streatham Vale had formerly been a narrow, muddy track: "On each side of the lane were fields of flowers, chrysanthemums and pansies, with large patches of turnips, mangold-wurzel, carrots and other root crops."[1] "A Cottage Tenant" remembered "the unlighted fields and market gardens" of Lonesome.[2] Around Manor Road, to the south-east, Constance Pope remembered fields of pansies and vegetables, as well as elm trees and pastures for cattle.[3] A columnist, The Commoner, (admittedly a writer of habitually nostalgic or reactionary temper) recalled, after house-building had begun, how he once liked to "saunter along rutted but shady Manor-lane" and view "the blaze of summer glory provided by several of the finest cottage gardens in Mitcham".[4] In the fine summer of 1926 potential buyers of the first houses in Long Thornton were shown "a magnificent picture of rolling green fields, with pretty houses nestling in the glorious sunshine".[5]

By the 1920s Lonesome's industry was well established. The chemical works of Messrs Forster and Gregory produced pigments and solvents, some of which were hazardous and obnoxious, for the India rubber industry;[6] established in 1852, it lasted until the mid-1930s, when the six-acre site was used for the completion of Rowan Crescent.

Lonesome in the 1920s might be defined as the inhabited and partly industrialised area south of the end of Streatham Vale and north of Meopham Road, with playing fields to the west and market gardens extending to Eastfields. At least until the 1890s the area, and the lane to Streatham, had a reputation as a place to be avoided, even in daylight, by unaccompanied women and children.[7] Gipsies used the route to and from Mitcham, and some Streatham residents thought of people from Mitcham as rough.[8] By 1913 Lonesome had been reached by motor-bus,[9] and the London General company began a local service from The Greyhound to Lonesome in 1921.

Though isolated, Lonesome was nevertheless the only named habitation close to the building sites that soon replaced many of the fields, the easiest point of location for land purchasers and for local newspapers. Eastfields had its level crossing over the railway, its market gardens and Pain's firework factory; workers lived in cottages nearby, in Acacia Road, Tamworth Lane and Manor Road, but Lonesome, through its suggestive name, caught the ear and initially defined a new suburb.

The area stopped being lonesome when rows of houses were built along and to the sides of the thoroughfare renamed Streatham Vale in 1924,[10] and over the clay-soil fields to the east and south-east,[a] where

---

a) Compare the maps on pp. 31 and 102 in Montague.

similar houses began to line Constance Pope's Manor Road and where another pioneer settlement took its name from that of the field on which it was built: Long Thornton Park.

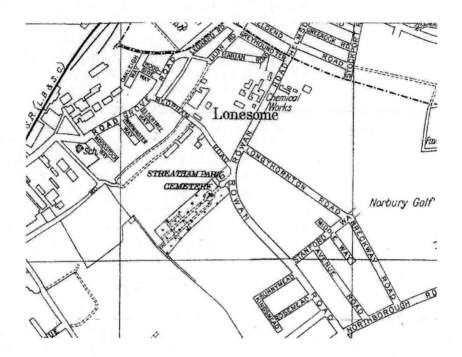

Lonesome in late 1927, before the building of the mission church: the Long Thornton Park estate is bottom right; the Meads are laid out, but not built; Wates housing is along and off Grove Road. (Map published by Crofts & Co.)

Long Thornton Park was but one of the estates around London built either by private speculative builders or by municipal authorities, notably the London County Council.[a] South London was expanding rapidly: the Government was encouraging new housing through subsidies, and within the area south of the Thames covered by the Church of England's Diocese of Southwark the population rose by 7.3% between 1921 and 1931 and a population shift of 300,000 was expected both from inner-city parishes and by migration from other areas. To provide new churches and social centres in rootless districts became the great challenge for the Church, one to which the Southwark Diocese rose with an impressive show of administration and money-raising in the Twenty-five Churches Fund.

Appointed to the See of Southwark in 1919, Cyril Forster Garbett found a diocese where slum housing abounded and where many of the clergy were demoralised. He set about raising funds to improve the pay and conditions of parish clergy to a level that would no longer inhibit recruitment, visited all his parishes and then set about the provision of churches for the new estates, meanwhile acquiring a knowledge of inner-city housing that allowed him to campaign in print and in the House of Lords for improvement.[1]

In autumn 1925 he launched a five-year appeal for £100,000 for the Twenty-five Churches Fund (well over £4m by today's values). The Bishop was determined that, when people moved into their new homes on the estates, the Church should be there to welcome them. As new estates were built, priests were to be appointed and plans laid down for churches, halls and vicarages when sites were found.

The Bishop and his treasurer, Brigadier-General E. B. Cuthbertson, addressed meetings across the diocese to seek donations. In February 1926, at the Mansion House, the Archbishop of Canterbury, Randall Davidson, spoke in support of Bishop Garbett's efforts. A week of prayer and self-denial in November 1927 culminated in a thanksgiving service at which gifts totalling £19,000 were presented. After only three years the appeal ended on 27 June 1928, when the Bishop sat in the cathedral to receive offerings from a never-ending stream of people, and the target was reached. Bishop Garbett recalled the cheering and clapping as he left the cathedral as "one of the great moments of my life".[2]

Grants from the Fund might be directed to new Districts to build at least a hall where no form of church building existed, or disbursed upon

---

a) The estate along the stretch of Northborough Road that is within the London Borough of Croydon is an LCC estate begun before the First World War.

application from local building committees and church councils. Congregations, already established or newly formed, were expected to raise funds locally before the Fund would make substantial contributions beyond any initial setting-up grant. About half the churches of the Twenty-five were enlargements of extant buildings or built where there had before been a congregation in a temporary building. Grants towards permanent buildings depended on how much could be raised locally or from grants; the City Parochial Charities Fund was particularly generous in its contributions towards suburban churches. A few churches, such as St Barnabas, Downham, had one or more considerable benefactions from private donors; The Holy Redeemer, Streatham Vale, had support from funds earlier accumulated towards an unbuilt memorial to the members of the early nineteenth-century Clapham Sect; on the other hand, St Michael, East Wickham, with very little local money, was supported by £8,000 from the Fund. St Olave, Mitcham, was unique in being largely funded through the sale of the site of a redundant church.

Even before the Fund began, the Diocese of Southwark had paid for a temporary church on the LCC estate of 2,000 dwellings at Bellingham, and the permanent church there was the first to benefit from the Fund. Municipal estates were large and took time to plan, so that the Church had plenty of warning of where churches would be needed and could participate in the development of estates. Sites were purchased early on for Bellingham, as well as for Downham (6,000 dwellings) and Middle Park, Eltham (2,000 dwellings). Territorial wrangling delayed and partly thwarted Bishop Garbett's plans for the giant LCC estate at St Helier.

Very few, if any, of Southwark's inter-war churches, apart from those on the municipal estates, were built in green-field locations such as the estates of Streatham Vale, Long Thornton Park and Manor Road, where Lonesome was the only adjacent settlement and the Good Shepherd Mission in Lilian Road the only outpost of the Church of England. The speed at which private companies formed themselves and built houses, with the ready consent of local planning authorities, perhaps explains what might seem to be a delay in having churches ready for the new residents. In the London Borough of Wandsworth, work began on private houses in and around Streatham Vale in 1924, and on the hall of The Holy Redeemer in 1927; in the Urban District of Mitcham the Council knew by April 1925 of an intended Long Thornton estate and approved the proposals of Fulfords and the Crematorium Company in March 1926,[3] but the mission church was not ready until early 1928.

3: THE MISSION CHURCH

Speaking at a meeting in support of the Twenty-five Churches Fund, held in June 1926 in Carshalton, the Bishop of Southwark cited the area with the "gloomy name of Lonesome", where contractors had purchased fields where they intended to build houses for 24,000 [sic] people within three years. Houses became available for occupation in September 1926,[1] but it was not until a year later, by which time seven hundred houses had been taken over by their buyers,[1] that the Vicar of St Mark, Mitcham, within whose parish the new houses lay, sought permission from the Urban District Council to build a parish hall, church and vicarage on a site to be purchased from Fulfords Ltd, the developers of Long Thornton Park. Fulfords had asked the UDC in April if land not allocated for dwellings could be used for a church and later suggested a clergy-house too; no objections were made, and the Twenty-five Churches Fund paid £500 for the transfer of the land on 17 October 1927.[2]

The site, at about 1½ acres, offered more than ample space for the three buildings eventually built, so much that in 1968 the then Vicar described much of the land as "merely wasted".[3] The pre-1976 spacious grounds are still fondly recalled by some residents, probably unaware of the labour involved in maintaining a space that was not always respected by those who saw it as a public one. The price asked may represent some act of generosity on the part of the vendors; at about the same time, Fulfords paid £1,850 for a slightly smaller area for house-building in Long Thornton Road,[2] and the site for church, hall and parsonage at Downham cost at least £1,000 in 1925–6. However, it is also possible that the price was low because the land could not be used for dwellings; in February Fulfords had had a scheme for 161 houses "at Long Thornton" turned down by the UDC because of non-compliance with the Town Planning Scheme, and it was also because of Ministry of Health stipulations about housing density that the site of the Ratepayers' Association sports ground became available.

Perhaps the need to catch up with the completion of homes influenced the type of construction used for the new mission centre; perhaps cheapness was a priority. Chart, Son and Reading, a well-established Mitcham firm of surveyors and architects, designed a building, to be erected by the Merton Abbey Joinery Works, of simple construction. Asbestos sheeting formed the cladding on a timber frame, whilst the roof was tiled in red asbestos. A boarded ceiling covered the main space, sized fifty feet by thirty feet, and a narrower space formed the 'sanctuary'. Heating was by gas radiators. A vestry and a kitchen completed the building. The cost, probably around £1,500,[b] was borne by the Twenty-five Churches Fund.

The 'sanctuary' space could be screened off, though the 'nave' was not often used for purely social purposes during the building's designation as a mission church. Over 250 seats[c] were provided; even if such a number was not normally required, Revd H. Coxwell White nevertheless told the Southwark Diocesan Conference in November 1928 that the building was so crowded that it would soon prove inadequate.

Church furnishings arrived as gifts from individuals or from older parishes; a missionary priest, Revd R. K. Haslam, was appointed on 7 November 1927, and the Bishop of Southwark dedicated the building on 26 January 1928. From Christmas 1927 until the new mission church could be used, services were held in the Good Shepherd Mission Room.

In the first issue of the church magazine Fr Haslam explained that the new District would be called "St Olave's" and that the permanent parish church would also be so dedicated. "In order that we can have a permanent church here sooner than would otherwise have been possible, the Bishop has very kindly earmarked the money from the sale of the site of St Olave, Southwark,[d] towards this purpose. The adoption of the name of St Olave is one of the conditions of the money being employed for his object."[e] He also reprinted an extract from a London County Council report of 1918 to explain the identity and history of the patron saint.[f]

---

b) This is an estimate: the same builders in 1930 erected a temporary hall at St Luke, Northover, and a mission hut in Arras Avenue, St Helier; the former, smaller than the Mitcham building, cost £1,500 plus furnishings.[8]

c) The number in the first edition of the parish magazine is 400, quoted by Richardson. An Ecclesiastical Commissioners' report of 17/03/31 gives 350. The capacity recorded in *SDD* 1929–30 is 200 (though there is a chance that this figure is simply a carry-over from the previous year's figure for the Good Shepherd Mission Room). Illustration 4 shows 8 seats per side, and even at A. C. Martin's ungenerous allowance per person for the new church, the main congregation area, with space for a gangway, could not have had many more than about 200 seats, to which would be added the forty or so occupants of the choir and sanctuary spaces. See Mrs Bulbeck's comment p. 26 on the "small" hall.

d) For the history of this church, see Appendix A.

e) There is no extant written evidence of this stipulation, though it would have been an understandable request from the Trustees of St Olave, Southwark. The LCC had also wanted the name preserved.

f) See Appendix C.

Two months after the dedication service, the Bishop recalled the occasion as being among his "hours of special joy", a contrast to the difficulties created by the rejection of the revised Prayer Book by Parliament. He recalled the crowd there, "notwithstanding a pouring wet night and a quagmire of mud in unfinished roads".[4] The Bishop expressed to Fr Haslam his surprise that a choir had been formed in so short a time and the local press noted the good congregation present and the "full and solemn service". The first Sunday services took place on 29 January.

After the initial crowd the first services, according to Deaconess Edith Todhunter, were attended by a small but devoted body of worshippers and a large, enthusiastic choir. She recalled, too, the peculiar difficulty of the unmade roads, and "heroic journeys in the early dark mornings, or still darker evenings". She, as did other commentators in the early days of Long Thornton, had to search far and wide for expressions to convey the conditions: "We imagined ourselves in Western Canada as we swayed to and fro on floating sleepers, or ploughed our way through thick clay, often leaving our galoshes behind." With minor internal alterations the mission church fulfilled its purpose until the consecration of the permanent church: the musical instruments used for the accompaniment of services changed, and the pulpit was replaced by the one (minus base and stairs) from St Olave, Southwark. Church groups met in the main hall or in the vestry. Though the building was "regarded as only a temporary one", the same report described it as "substantially built" and "not of the 'tin tabernacle' style".

Soon after the opening of the mission church, Fr Haslam found himself in dispute with residents concerning the public use of the cinder-path established between Middle Walk (now Middle Road) and Long Thornton Road for the use of worshippers. One of his arguments was the damage that could easily be done to the temporary building. That damage, deliberate or otherwise, was done may be inferred from a resolution in 1930 to replace the vestry windows with plywood rather than glass, whilst later, in 1932, the locks of the hall were overhauled and the main doors fastened by a bar inside.[g]

After several years of heavy and sometimes rough use the Church Council agreed in 1937 to redecorate the hall inside and out and to install new stage lighting. Despite this fresh start, misuse of the hall interior by Boy Scouts led to breakages.

On the outbreak of war in 1939 the hall was requisitioned and used as a British Restaurant. It had a small part in the history of British television when Alan Simpson, once a boy in the choir at St Olave's and later famous as half of a scriptwriting partnership, wrote and performed

g) The hall was not the only target in 1930–2: trees newly planted in the streets were damaged, as was the Ratepayers' sports ground.

entertainments on its stage.[5] In 1943 an appeal began to replace the "inadequate and unsuitable" accommodation when peacetime conditions returned; peacetime proved to be as financially difficult as wartime, so the hall remained, even though its fabric was beyond revival, "in a bad way" in 1949 and "in poor condition" by 1970. Once the land on which it stood had been sold for housing, the building that had been "the scene of worship, social activities and entertainment since the parish was first formed"[6] suffered an ignominious end in 1976, being "completely wrecked by children who live in the roads around the church".[7]

It may be worth wondering what effect the choice of structure had on the later years of the parish. Over half of the Twenty-five churches began as dual-purpose buildings, but all except three were brick-built and most of these were still standing in 2002. Nearby, The Holy Redeemer parish has a good example of a hall designed by a well-known architect, Sir Charles Nicholson; this hall cost over £4,000, as did that at St Barnabas, Downham, neither of which was fully funded from the Twenty-five Churches Fund. The Twenty-five Churches Fund could pay in full (£1,500–£2,000) for a less substantial building; it was, as Fr Haslam pointed out, to that fund that "we are entirely indebted for our mission church." To have presented a barely-arrived congregation with debt would surely have hindered the effort soon made in fund-raising for a permanent church.

However, had the St Olave's hall/church been a more solid structure, it would probably not have needed replacing in the 1970s, and the church would not have become so hemmed in by other structures. The land sale paid to replace the hall, but did not have the effect on church finance that was sought; though it is possible, with hindsight, to find fault with some of the 1970s scheme and its consequences, the problem it had to solve was created in 1927.

4: THE TRUE, AUTHENTIC MARK OF PRIESTHOOD

The establishment of churches and halls in the new Districts around South London was a priority for the Bishop of Southwark, who knew his clergy well and carefully selected the priests to take on this special missionary work.[1] Revd Reginald Kingdon Haslam, the first Vicar of St Olave, Mitcham, was a missionary priest, first in deprived parts of South London and then among the newly arrived population of Long Thornton; it was for missionary work in South Africa that he left the parish he had formed and led with "experienced guidance" and "remarkable enthusiasm"; in wartime Surbiton he ministered to a congregation with neither church nor hall.

Fr Haslam arrived in Long Thornton in his early forties with the usual clergy education of university and theological college, experience of parish work in Wandsworth and Walworth, a brief experience as a chaplain in the First World War and a strength of character that had survived a dreadful event in his family life. One of the several tributes to his work will suffice as an introduction:

During the ten years he has been in Long Thornton, he has seen church work in the district grow from very modest beginnings to its present flourishing scale. To his enterprise, backed by the cordial support of his congregation and the Church authorities, is due the really magnificent church which is now at the centre of religious life on the estate, and there are several other channels through which he has impressed his personality on the district.

Reginald Kingdon Haslam was born on Christmas Day 1885 at Knighton, Leicestershire, the first child of Revd Herbert Kingdon Haslam and his wife, Florence. The "Kingdon" came from Herbert Haslam's mother, born Mary Delia Kingdon. Herbert Haslam seems to have had a somewhat unsettled career in the Church; until his last appointment, he stayed barely more than four years in any one place. After his ordination he served briefly at St Nicholas, Sutton, and came back to that place for a year in 1895–6 as a voluntary second curate at Christ Church, Sutton,[2] whose Vicar later advised Fr Haslam on musical matters and probably recommended his own college, St John's, Cambridge, as a place for university education.

During the 1895–6 stay in Sutton Reginald Haslam attended Sutton Park School, "the oldest established school in Sutton ... preparatory for Public Schools".[3] Thereafter he was educated at home for three years before becoming a boarder until 1902 at Stamford School in Lincolnshire, some thirty miles from his father's then parish of Wold [now Old] in Northamptonshire.

The next five years are empty of evidence of what Reginald Haslam was doing, though his younger brother went up to Cambridge in 1906. His father returned as a curate to Christ Church, Sutton, in September

1907, received as an "old friend"[4] by the Vicar there; he resigned his living at Wold and by the start of 1908 the family was domiciled in Sutton. The move involved many sacrifices, including reduction of income, but Herbert Haslam hoped to "obtain the comparative peace and quietness which he enjoyed on his previous visit."[2]

On 2 February 1908 Revd Herbert Haslam preached at Christ Church; on the next Sunday morning he locked himself into the bathroom at his home and attempted to cut his throat with a razor. After medical attention he was removed to the Bethlem Hospital and Asylum in Southwark; hopes for his recovery were entertained, but within the week he had died of septic pneumonia. Reginald Haslam gave evidence of identification to the inquest at Southwark and described finding his father; he testified that his father had been suffering from serious insomnia and worry over his ten-year-old daughter's prolonged and serious illness. The jury found that Herbert Haslam had committed suicide while of unsound mind.[5]

It is of course impossible to assess what effect such a catastrophe had on the deceased's family; one practical consequence some eighteen months later may have been that Reginald, the elder son, felt able or motivated to follow his younger brother to Cambridge. It is possible that he delayed furthering his education because of his father's health, which had been failing while at Wold—though he testified at the inquest to his father's normally good health.

Reginald Haslam became an undergraduate at St John's College, Cambridge, on 9 August 1909; he studied History, and, after a Third Class in his 1911 examinations, proceeded to the degree of Bachelor of Arts in 1912. Aside from this modest academic achievement, he took an active part in the college's Debating Society: after speaking in the Freshmen's debate in favour of the public school system, he moved to declaring himself in favour of the extension to women of voting rights (this in an era of militant actions by suffragettes); he spoke against the idea of a self-sufficient empire (what would later be called protectionism or empire preference); he sided with the legislation proposed after the two general elections of 1909 to restrict the rights of veto by the House of Lords.[6] In retrospect we might detect some 'progressive' views, and in later years Fr Haslam was described as "always outspoken in his opinions".

After Cambridge came a year of Theology at Ripon College, and Reginald Haslam was ordained Deacon on 28 September 1913 in Southwark Cathedral. He became a Missioner at the Pembroke College Mission, founded in 1885 by students from Pembroke College, Cambridge, to be a centre for social action in Walworth, and was ordained Priest in 1914. Several colleges at Oxford and Cambridge, as well as some public schools, founded missions in inner London: Fr Haslam's own college had one, also in Walworth, that may have been his introduction to work in poor areas. Poor urban parishes had been

10

since the 1860s the ones looked for by unmarried Anglo-Catholic clergy,[7] something that should be remembered to his credit when reading about the problems Fr Haslam encountered at St Olave's because of the Anglo-Catholic forms of worship that he brought with him.

Two years into the First World War, on 2 October 1916, Fr Haslam began service as an army chaplain at the Second Western General Hospital in Manchester. In September 1918 he was posted to France as Chaplain to the 47th Divisional Artillery, and after a brief experience of the Western Front was gazetted out of the Army as Honorary Chaplain to the Forces, Fourth Class, on 25 September 1919. The Assistant Chaplain General of the First Army noted of Fr Haslam that "he has done good work during the short time he has been in France" and that the work he wished to pursue was the "same as before (work in a London slum)". And so, for a while, he returned to Walworth.[8]

In August 1920 Fr Haslam became a curate in the non-slum parish of St Anne, Wandsworth. We cannot know the reason for his move, but a curacy would probably have been a required qualification for the later holding of a living as a Vicar or Rector. Revd Arthur Eglington,[a] the Vicar of St Anne's, wrote fulsomely of Fr Haslam's qualities when he came to leave after only a year: "We shall sorely miss him ... We shall remember that simpleness and goodness are the strongest elements in genuine Christian character." Two aspects of his ministry were specially commended: he visited many parishioners in their homes and he started the parish's activities for boys "on a really sound basis"; in Long Thornton he made visiting the foundation of his building up a congregation and very quickly recruited a boys' choir in time for the dedication of the mission church.

At Wandsworth, too, Fr Haslam experienced the reluctance of a congregation to accept changes in the practices of worship put forward by a priest who had only recently arrived in the parish, and a statement of principles published in the church magazine at St Anne's found its way almost word for word into the church magazine at St Olave's.[9]

After his year's curacy Fr Haslam returned to Walworth, but this time as Vicar of The Lady Margaret church in Chatham Street. The parish took its title from the founder of St John's College, Cambridge, following the establishment in 1883 of a college mission in Walworth, and the buildings consisted of a church, hostel and parsonage, designed by Ewan Christian.[10] His experience here of raising funds for repairs came in useful later; at Mitcham he certainly proved to have a clear grasp of all matters financial as they related to the growth of the parish.

---

a) Bishop Garbett included Eglington in a short list of "real giants" that he found at work in the Diocese of Southwark when he arrived in 1919.[19]

11

Appointed Missionary Priest[b] on 7 November 1927, by early December Fr Haslam had taken up residence in Long Thornton, lodging with Mr and Mrs Martin at 56 Stanford Way. From early 1930 until the vicarage was built he lived at 44 St Olave's Walk, purchased by the Ecclesiastical Commissioners and defined by them as a "temporary house of residence". From his lodgings Fr Haslam began the systematic visiting of the houses in the district that was the foundation of his work in Long Thornton and he met, according to the *News,* with "a very cordial welcome". Keeping in touch with the new population was a task that at times "proved too much even for his energies", and was still his "chief difficulty" in 1935–6.[11] Supervision of the building of the new church deprived him of a holiday in 1930, but in other years he travelled to Switzerland and to Cornwall. Besides private holidays, he seems happily to have conducted group visits for others: Switzerland in 1929 and 1936, and Cambridge in 1936.

Fr Haslam clearly enjoyed his participation in the camps for boys run in most summers, where one of his specialities was the organisation of nature study. The choir camp in 1934 at Blue Anchor in Somerset he called an "ideal holiday—dips in the sea, walks along the shore, shells and fossils, local places—time went all too quickly." After two weeks of invigorating air in 1928 he felt "refreshed once again for my work"; in a life "free from convention" he probably felt happy to leave behind the obligations of parish life and also to show sides of his personality not obvious in a more formal environment. One evening in 1928 he guided the group back to camp by candle-lamp across the dark open countryside[c] between Friday Street and Leith Hill.

Fr Haslam was perhaps an amateur conjuror or illusionist; after a group visit to Maskelyne and Devant's[d] in 1928 he noted that "the tricks baffled even those of us who have done a little experimenting in this way ourselves." Beyond such hints of a lighter or informal side, we know most about his personality through the high regard shown for his achievements; "sincerity", "deepest respect" and "definite views" are all included in Thornvale's valedictory comments, and his generosity towards the church was acknowledged, but we cannot tell if he was witty

---

b) The Lady Margaret parish in Walworth, Fr Haslam's parish, had a net value in 1929 of £400, whereas the Mission Church in Long Thornton was valued at £200. The Vicar of St Mark's, Mitcham, called this an "act of self-sacrifice". The stipend increased by £50 once the District became a Parish, and in 1936 the net value of the parish was £400 p.a. Mitcham Parish Church was worth £748. (*EC* 91151/1; *SDD*; *Advertiser* 08/09/27)

c) So described at the time, however wooded the area may now be.

d) Maskelyne and Devant had resident seasons in London; the shows featured elaborate stage illusions and special effects.

as well as earnest, or an easy conversationalist as well as a preacher. His successor's sociable qualities (and those of his wife) were soon noticed and recorded, which might imply that they differed from Fr Haslam's. At a parish party in 1939 Fr Haddelsey, "our most versatile Vicar" gave a marionette show: "such a human person" was the judgement in the parish magazine. The annual meeting of 1939 heard of the "many-sided personality" of the Vicar and his generous offering of the vicarage for meetings, as well as the "charm and support" of Mrs Haddelsey.

However much Fr Haddelsey and his wife shone in sociability, Fr Haslam was certainly not disliked, and his mission could not have succcccded without personal attraction. Thornvale in the *Advertiser* thought Fr Haslam was "one of a type of clergy which is needed in the Church today". The first curate praised his "tremendous sense of vocation" and recalled that "RK ... had a great gift for drawing people of the most varied backgrounds and temperaments into the life of the Church."[12] He was always held in the "highest esteem and respect" according to the souvenir programme for the 1938 St Nicholas Fayre; it recalled his "indefatigability, courage and excellent leadership and guidance", but also remembered "the band of willing helpers who gathered round him and gave him every assistance from the commencement". Such generous help would scarcely have been offered and sustained without some inspirational leadership from the missionary priest.

Fr Haslam gave freely to the church he served. He provided his own Mass vestments so that the parish did not have to pay (though that meant, less helpfully, that very few vestments were available for the use of the next Vicar). He did not retain the Easter Offering gifts made annually by the congregation, but gave the money, between £12 and £20 per year, to church funds, whilst he and his sister jointly donated £100 towards the new vicarage. As Dr Pailthorpe pointed out, "he was in no way called upon to give in such measure." The chest for the storage of altar frontals was given by him, and he himself made and gave the kneeling-rugs for the altar rails and sanctuary. When he left Mitcham, he gave a set of unbleached Mass vestments to St Olave's and funded the production by ladies of the parish of an altar frontal. Alone among the parishes where he served, St Olave's was remembered thirty years later in Fr Haslam's will, in which he bequeathed £1,000[e] to the parish.

The "definite views" mentioned by Thornvale can be seen in many sections of this history, as they relate to worship in church and the national controversy over the Prayer Book in 1927–8. He could certainly be sharp in his comments, as seen in the ritual controversy and the

---

e) Over £11,000 in purchasing power by 2010; six new gas heaters were bought in 1972 with his bequest and a gift from his sister.

replacement of the organist in 1930. His views on baptism were outspoken:[f] those parents that he met who wanted baptism, but did not otherwise intend to come to church services, he described as "baptised heathen". His preferred policy accorded with views that were approved within Anglo-Catholicism,[g] and when he was later publicly criticised we can see the divergence between his reforming desire for religious sincerity and the idea of christening as a social convention.

Though he did not court publicity in the local press, in national or local matters he sometimes issued challenges. In 1933 he commended the League of Nations Union for its advocacy of collective disarmament[h] and in November 1934 made what the *Advertiser* called "characteristic observations" about Christians and war:

The majority of people who live in this country today would be prepared to say that they do not believe in war, but as Christians, surely if we have the courage of our convictions we ought at least to consider, whether our Christian principles do not also compel us to say "I will not, therefore, take any part whatsoever in war or the preparation for it." No true pacifist is a coward and, even if he were, it is far better to be a self-admitted coward than a canting hypocrite who says that he does not believe in war yet regards war as an evil necessity and believes in it at any rate enough to say that, should another war arise, he would be prepared to take part in it.

When the Majestic cinema in Mitcham proposed to open on Sundays, several local clergy pronounced against the idea. Though Fr Haslam was not in favour, he did not join the campaign; he thought purely repressive measures were unwise and that the Church should show a better way, not prohibit alternatives: "Much of the present day apathy to religion is a direct result of establishing a Sabbatical observance of the Lord's Day." He had in 1929 supported local objections to the exclusive use of part of Mitcham Common by a golf club—it should be used by the people—and commented on the "mushroom growth" and lack of planning in the area: "It was inevitable where building on such a large scale is due to private and not to public enterprise." This may remind us that he had worked for years in deprived areas where the only new housing was provided either by charitable trusts or by local authorities. Though he had experienced the difficulties of life in Long Thornton before the roads were made up, he does not seem to have allied himself with the Ratepayers' Association; indeed, after a donation from the

---

f) See Chapter 18.

g) A speaker at the 1923 Anglo-Catholic Congress was greeted with cheers when he suggested a more rigorous policy about baptisms.[20]

h) See also Chapter 21.

Association in 1929 of £3 to the Church Building Fund, the two bodies went on their separate ways.

Ten years in one parish may have been long enough[i] for a man who wanted missionary challenge; Fr Haslam perhaps felt that he had done all he could. The achievements had been considerable, not least in financing a church, a vicarage and the beginnings of a new District; however, the latter items required the abandonment of his hopes to have the Lady Chapel built at St Olave's, and he had not relished the prospect of yet another fair to raise more money. In 1935–6 there were disputes over baptism policy, the introduction of a statue of Our Lady and the use of incense, but most of the arguments over Anglo-Catholic worship seemed to have been won by 1938 (even "Father" as a title was now used, if only in writing). After 1936 the parish was of a more manageable size, but the congregation at St Olave's decreased as worshippers living in the District of The Ascension went to the new hall/church there. The loss by the end of 1937 of valuable church workers through removals from the district may have disheartened him a little: in some reflections after his first ten years he noted that it had "not always been easy or even possible to find others who are ready to step forward to fill up the gaps ... but still the work goes on." He looked back with pleasure to the early days of the mission church, hard work but satisfying.[j]

Two of his curates had gone on to missionary work abroad, and this was the path Fr Haslam chose. He left St Olave's with little public advertisement and "slipped away quietly ... with no valedictory speech-making" in the last week of January 1938, as he had announced in the January magazine. However, he did not leave completely for some time; after a holiday in Switzerland he officiated at a 7 a.m. Mass, signed the services register for the last time as Vicar on 25 February and left for South Africa.

The South African expedition proved a sad disappointment. He was licensed to officiate by the Bishop of Grahamstown in 1938,[13] but in a letter from St Mary's Rectory in Port Elizabeth that arrived in England in time for the June church magazine he expressed much discontent: he had not settled down, even after two months, and was not doing the sort of work that he went to South Africa to do; it might be some time before that was possible. In October 1938 he was reported to be returning to England.

---

i) This was a view he himself expressed in 1954 when he left St Mark, Surbiton.

j) Probably insignificantly, after a tiring year in 1936 his holiday was curtailed by a car crash that led to hospital treatment for two broken ribs.

By 1940 he was a curate in Basingstoke.[k] He had not forgotten St Olave's: he attended Evensong at the Feast of Dedication in 1942 and contributed a generous obituary for William Carey, the Verger, to the church magazine. In October 1943 he became the Curate-in-Charge of St Mark, Surbiton. This was certainly a missionary challenge: the church had been gutted by high-explosive and incendiary bombs on 2 October 1940 and there was no church hall; Sunday services were held in the hall of Surbiton Boys' Grammar School, and weekday ones in the drawing-room of the vicarage. It was not at all certain that the Diocese of Southwark wanted the parish to retain its identity. Fr Haslam seems to have been just the man for the job: during the difficult war years "his cheerful face and voice soon became known to Surbiton at large and to the parish in particular," and his efforts to hold together and direct his parishioners, "keeping alive and bright their vision of the time to come", were remembered years later.[14] The *Surrey Comet* recorded that he had "earned praise for his inspiring leadership".[15] Canon J. Halet, who was Vicar until 1943, wrote in 1955 that "as a visitor and money-raiser, under great difficulties, [Fr Haslam] was surely remarkable"—though he also recalled that "he had his oddities, like the rest of us."[16]

Fr Haslam persuaded the Diocese that it would be right to build a temporary church and raised funds for this after the war, partly through gift days. He commissioned plans from A. C. Martin (the St Olave's architect) for a new permanent structure, generally similar to the old one, and showed them to the Annual Meeting in February 1946.[17] The temporary church was built and survives as the church hall, but a different architect rebuilt St Mark's after Fr Haslam's departure. He evidently continued his personal generosity: when presented with a cheque before he left the parish, he was asked to use it for himself, not to plough it back into the church.

On 3 November 1954 Fr Haslam was instituted as Rector of Aller with Pitney-Lortie, near Langport in Somerset. He told parishioners in Surbiton that he was looking for more pioneering work, not an easier parish; even in 1954 vacancies in rural parishes were becoming hard to fill. However, he was now nearly seventy; his age shows in the farewell photograph in the *Surrey Comet*,[18] but the challenge of the new work was at least not one of numbers, since the populations were now in hundreds, not thousands.

After retirement in 1958 Fr Haslam died on 26 January 1971 in Weston-super-Mare.

---

k) This may be explained by the translation in 1932 of Bishop Garbett, late of the Diocese of Southwark, to Winchester, in which diocese Basingstoke lies. Coincidentally, in 1928 St Mark, Surbiton, gave some fittings to the mission church in Mitcham.

5: WORSHIP 1928–39

The magazine of December 1927 announced this pattern of services:

Sundays:

Holy Communion: 8 a.m., 9 a.m.
Holy Communion (sung, with address): 10 a.m.
(1st and 3rd) Plain Holy Communion Service: 10 a.m.
Mattins and Litany: 9.30 a.m.
Evensong and Sermon: 6.30 p.m.

Weekdays:

Wednesday 6.30 p.m.	Holy Communion
Daily 9 a.m.	Mattins
5.30 p.m.	Evensong (Saturdays, 7.30 p.m.)

Holy Baptism: Sunday 4 p.m., Friday 7.30 p.m.

Churchings:[a] Sunday 4 p.m. and 9 a.m. daily.

Timings changed: the Sunday morning said services became earlier, and the main service, "sung with sermon", settled to the common time of 11 a.m., but the pattern remained during most of the pre-war period. The plain service was dropped after three months, and a sung Mattins made a brief appearance, until it, too, was discontinued because of poor attendances, though Mattins was still said before the main service on Sundays. On weekdays Morning and Evening Prayer were said daily. The weekday Holy Communion service became a daily one in 1932 when Fr Haslam first had the assistance of a curate. In 1938 the new Vicar inserted a People's Communion service at 9.30 a.m. on Sundays.

The 1927 services were all as prescribed by the Book of Common Prayer, the only legally permitted form of public worship in the Church of England. "Holy Communion" is the supplementary title for "The Lord's Supper"; "Mattins" is Morning Prayer and "Evensong" is Evening Prayer. However, from the first Sunday in the mission church the main service was not Morning Prayer, but Holy Communion, often in Anglo-Catholic churches called "Mass", in which "the sacrificial aspect of the Eucharist

---

a) More formally called "The Thanksgiving of Women after Child-Birth": it was once the common custom that women should go to church to give thanks for "safe deliverance", but this service has disappeared as the use of the Book of Common Prayer has declined and as childbirth has become safer than it was.

is emphasised, music and vestments with a rich ceremonial are used to make the service a great offering of praise and thanksgiving."[1] Normally, only the infirm might receive the sacrament at the main service; the devout churchgoer was expected to do so at an early morning service while still abstaining from food and drink, and to return to church later for the Sung service, there to be "lost in wonder, love and praise".[2] It must be supposed that at least some members of Fr Haslam's first congregations were already used to, or at least understood, this fasting communion arrangement, for otherwise it is hard to see how a practice followed in only a part of the Church of England could have been immediately established. Even so, it seems fairly clear that the Sung Eucharist was attended by many who did not receive the sacrament.[b]

From Christmas 1932 the festival was observed with a midnight service; communicants had to observe a six-hour rule of abstinence beforehand and notify the Vicar that they intended to receive the sacrament. Well over a hundred did so in that first year. Figures were purchased in 1931–2 for a Christmas crib. Fr Haslam was quite clear in 1928 that there would be no Watch Night service on New Year's Eve; no reason was given, but such things had come to be associated with Nonconformist and Low Anglican churches.

From 1928, Ante-Communion was said on the morning of Good Friday, with a Three Hours Service from midday. Possibly from 1930 and certainly by 1932 confessions were heard on the evening of Good Friday. On Easter Day two early Communion services were added, and the day ended with "Evensong, anthem and sermon". Ascension Day, always a Thursday, was marked with a sung Holy Communion service at 6.30 a.m. and Evensong at 6.30 p.m. In the late 1930s, breakfast after the morning service became the custom.

Corpus Christi, or thanksgiving for Holy Communion, and also a Thursday, merited a Holy Communion service at 6.30 a.m., by 1935 a sung one. From January 1936 a Requiem Mass was said on monthly Saturdays.

Harvest Festival, observed in the Church of England from the 1850s onwards, though not found in the Prayer Book, proved to be "bright and attractive to large congregations" in 1929. In most of the pre-war years this service took place on a weekday evening, with a visiting preacher. The cash collections at harvest were often larger than usual, which suggests that people outside the usual congregation attended.[3] Fr Haslam was not enthusiastic: he suggested, in vain, money in lieu of decorations and thought that much that was given was wasted by being left in church too long and because hospitals, even then, could not give the produce to patients.

---

b) See further discussion in Chapters 12 and 18.

Fr Haslam's successor[c] made confession a more publicly acknowledged sacrament, with advertised times before Christmas and Easter. He added a 9.30 a.m. Parish [or People's] Communion and thereby followed a trend advocated in a book published only four years earlier; this "encouraging sign of the times"[4] had barely begun when war altered the conditions for worship for years to come.

---

c) Charles Vincent Bernard Haddelsey, 1903–1994. After curacies at Long Eaton (Derbys.) and St Agnes, Kennington Park, he was Priest-in-Charge of St Alban, Ventnor, before becoming Vicar of St Olave's 1938–50. He then became Vicar of Syston (Leics.) 1950–9; Rector, Stratton Audley 1959–63; Vicar of South Ascot 1963–8; Warden, Leicester Diocese Retreat House from 1968.

When Fr Haslam announced his intentions for the services to be conducted in the mission church, he accepted that some would be alarmed because he had come from a High church, but declared: "No one who really knows me would call me an extremist. I would say quite frankly that I welcome the new Prayer Book. I do so, largely because of the very Christian spirit of toleration that I find all through its pages." His arrival in Long Thornton coincided with proposals put before Parliament by the Church of England to authorise changes to the Book of Common Prayer of 1662, and his welcome for the proposed new Book (though it was shared by the Prime Minister),[1] far from being a reassurance to anyone suspicious of his provenance and purpose, placed him on the side of those who, as many MPs thought, were trying to undermine "the Protestants, the old-fashioned believers in the Church of England".[2] Fr Haslam's first magazine article is dated 12 December 1927; amid scenes of great excitement the House of Commons rejected the proposed Book on 15 December.

Since the sixteenth century the Monarch in Parliament had prescribed the words that an English subject must use in public worship.[a] By 1927 Parliament had the right to approve or reject Measures proposed by the Church Assembly, but it could not engage in amendments.[3] Despite the protracted war of words between opposed church groups[b] and the organised lobbying of MPs by Protestant organisations, no one seems to have expected the House of Commons actually to use its right of rejection; the London *Evening Standard* thought that, after approval by the Lords, "a similar result may be anticipated with fair confidence."

The new book was intended to enrich the worship of the Church by providing new materials and alternative versions of the old services. It responded to the public need for remembrance during and after the First World War with prayers for the dead, once deemed unscriptural and Roman Catholic, but authorised in 1917; the baptism service was less insistent on the sinfulness of the child to be baptised; a bride could omit "obey" from her vows. These were moves towards the "reality" of post-war England, some acknowledgement that the Church had been "out of touch with the thoughts and ideas of the time".[4]

The revised service of Holy Communion, in using ideas from the Prayer Book of 1549 and from the Orthodox Church, broke away from

---

a) By 1927 different arrangements applied to the other three parts of the United Kingdom.

b) The Protestant objectors were united, and supported by the modernist Bishop of Birmingham, Dr Barnes, but Anglo-Catholics were divided.

the wilfully Protestant rite of Cranmer's 1552 book, and the new book also allowed priests, under licence from a bishop, to reserve portions of the bread and wine consecrated during a public service for use in bringing communion to the sick. Protestant groups saw the new Holy Communion service as an acceptance by the Church of England of doctrines of the Roman Catholic Church and opposed reservation because, if the sick could be so comforted, there must be some kind of real presence of Christ in the consecrated bread and wine, an opinion that they could never accept, within the Holy Communion service or outside it. Even worse, they feared that people might then start to adore the reserved sacrament as the Body and Blood of Christ, either in private devotion or in unauthorised services such as Benediction.

Some well-publicised campaigners emphasised the identity of Protestantism with national greatness: Bishop Knox, the retired Bishop of Manchester, thought that God willed England to be the leader among the Protestant nations, whilst one group of objectors to the new book claimed that revision would be "the first step in the rapid subjugation of England to the power of Rome".[5] Suspicion of the Pope and all things Roman Catholic had been bred into the English since the burnings of Queen Mary's reign; generations had been brought up with a knowledge of Foxe's *Book of Martyrs* and of the defeat of Catholic Spain's Armada by Protestant England.

The new book was meant to allow many by then commonplace practices within the Church of England. However, the bishops also wanted to demonstrate that there were to be clear boundaries beyond which clergy would not be allowed to go in following Roman Catholic practices: "The purpose of the revision project was to provide peace <u>and</u> order,"[6] an "ordered liberty".[7] Toleration within defined limits was indeed a feature of the book, but toleration was not a principle accepted by the book's opponents, particularly the lawyers, such as the Home Secretary, who wanted to "bring these illegal men [Anglo-Catholic priests] into line with the law".[8]

On the night of 15 December the opposition had a "complete oratorical superiority".[9] "No one concerned in the presentation of the case ... could grip his audience,"[10] whereas Rosslyn Mitchell, an anti-Catholic Scot, with "eloquence that moves a nation",[11] and the Home Secretary, Sir William Joynson-Hicks, persuaded the Commons to reject the book by 240 votes to 207.[c] There was prolonged cheering as the results were read.

Six months later, after the addition of stricter rules on reservation[d] (which only served to lose Anglo-Catholic support), the same thing

---

c) Figures from Maiden, p. 157; there was some confusion among the tellers on the night of the vote.

d) These were drafted by the Bishop of Southwark.[18]

happened again, this time by 268 votes to 222, despite a closing plea for the new book from Mr Baldwin, the Prime Minister. Another lawyer, Sir Thomas Inskip, made a substantial contribution to the defeat. The *Daily News* detected a hardening of opinion in the country.

After the 1927 defeat Fr Haslam was conciliatory and thought it premature to assume that Parliament wanted to define the Church's doctrines, but the Bishop of Southwark, in the monthly *Southwark Diocesan Gazette* that was included in the church magazine, wrote of the great humiliation that the Church had received from the State.[12] After the second vote Fr Haslam supported the Archbishop of Canterbury's statement that the Church should decide its own forms of worship: "She is God's new creation, not the creation of man or the State, and not subject to the authority and will of man or of the State, but of God." He wrote disparagingly of the "Home Secretary and his friends" and their "contriving" and criticised the view of some MPs that the Church Assembly was not truly representative.

The Bishop of Southwark in July 1928 deplored the "indiscriminate attacks" made on Anglo-Catholics and argued that limits in doctrine and worship must not be too finely drawn; a year later he wrote that the Anglo-Catholic movement "possesses a remarkable vitality and has evoked the enthusiasm of many who have been quite untouched by other sides of the life of our Church." Such comments were probably not welcome among those unhappy with Fr Haslam's introduction of Anglo-Catholic forms of worship. However, even as Bishop Garbett was deploring the intense dislike of Anglo-Catholicism that became evident in both debates, he acknowledged the justice of one kind of complaint, the "inconsiderateness" of some clergy that had emptied once-crowded churches.[13] It is possible to see this concern behind his refusal to sanction the use of incense at St Olave's.

In Mitcham the local papers showed no interest, though the *News* published a comment from the Vicar of Mitcham, Revd C. Aubrey Finch, who said that the 1927 debate showed "the strong hold which religion has in the heart of the nation", and it printed a list of how local MPs had voted in the 1928 debate.[e]

Parishioners could also read about the issues in their daily newspapers: the cheaper ones[f] showed no enthusiasm for the rejections

---

e) The Member for Mitcham voted with the Noes; in 1927 he was absent, unpaired, [*Hansard*] which suggests that, if he had received correspondence from constituents lobbying against the Book, as did many MPs, he did not feel concerned enough to act on it.

f) The *Daily Express* and the *Daily Mail* had circulations of around one million, the others rather less.

of the Book, even when, like the *Daily Sketch,* they printed a picture of the Home Secretary surrounded by congratulatory telegrams "after his Prayer Book triumph". Reactions were of sympathy for the Archbishop of Canterbury, of concern for the constitutional consequences and the possibility of separation of Church from State, and disapproval of the voting against the book by non-Anglicans and by Members with seats outside England.g The *Daily Mirror* praised those who had "laboured to effect a compromise that need exclude no reasonable religious view from the Church of the 'Middle Way'."[14] Prior to the votes in Parliament newspapers did not campaign against the proposed book; if there is in them a discernible general view, it is in favour of the toleration praised by Fr Haslam. Nevertheless, parishioners could not but notice the attention drawn to Anglo-Catholics in the Press and by some MPs. The *Daily Express*'s editorial thought that "the people of this country will cling to their Protestantism" and that "Anglo-Catholics have won many concessions", but, even so, commended the "comprehensiveness" of the Church of England.[15]

Some MPs seem to have taken up a role as defenders of the ordinary person against an ineffectual Church hierarchy that was betraying the British citizen's birthright. The *Daily News* in 1928 noted the "anti-clericalism" of some Labour Members who interrupted when bishops were mentioned. It is just possible that this opposition of Lords and Commons had a counterpart in Long Thornton, where Fr Haslam was almost certainly the only Cambridge MA in a parish of clerks and artisans.

Plainness certainly did become an issue in Long Thornton. During the ritual dispute at St Olave's in 1930 "One of the Plain People" wrote to the *News*: "We, the 'plain people', are quite satisfied with the way the services were conducted before the advent of the Anglo-Catholics *and the new Prayer Book.*"[16] One man who had left St Olave's recalled the Bishop of Woolwich's promise that St Olave's would be "a church for the people". In the early days "the services were of a simple character. It was the plain service such as would meet the wishes of average people." Another correspondent lamented that "people of simple tastes and belief" had joined the church and found later that the services became "almost of Roman Catholic type". His claim that "much has been done to turn people away" through the form of the services echoed complaints heard in Parliament.

It is hard to know if the Prayer Book controversy made Fr Haslam's establishment of a church with Catholic leanings any more difficult than it would have been anyway; he soon started using the new form of Evening Prayer, but it was the lack of consultation with his Church

---

g) Had only MPs from English constituencies voted, the measure would have been passed by 199 to 175. The parliamentary issue here prefigures Tam Dalyell's 1977 West Lothian Question.

Council that caused disquiet, as much as the book itself. Those who expected Fr Haslam to be an "ordinary Church of England man" found that he was challenging what they expected "church" to be. "I am certainly an Anglo-Catholic; I have never desired to be otherwise," he told the *News*. Anglo-Catholics were indeed different; they were not a comfortable *status quo*. As an organiser of the 1920 Anglo-Catholic Congress[h] said: "We desire above all things to publish plainly and distinctly the good things of the Catholic Faith and the Christian religion."[17]

---

h) Described as "spectacular" in *ODCC*, five such events were held in London and elsewhere in 1920–33. The Congresses held in London could not be easily ignored: in 1920 the queue for the closing service in Southwark Cathedral stretched across London Bridge and hundreds could not gain entry; the 1923 Congress began with a Sung Eucharist in St Paul's Cathedral and ended with a procession of priests and bishops across Trafalgar Square to St Martin-in-the-Fields; audiences of four thousand filled the Albert Hall during the week of the 1927 Congress.[19]

7: THE RITUAL DISPUTE OF 1930

In December 1930 "a gentleman who takes a prominent part in public as well as church affairs" [almost certainly Councillor Field] wrote in the *News* that "the form of service in the mission church has undergone violent and rapid change in ritual and is now almost of Roman Catholic type." More specific complaints were:

- Holy Communion is now called Mass[a]
- special honour is given the Virgin Mary
- the confessional has been introduced
- frequent processions, with the use of candles and robes
- incense will be used in the new church.

One resident complained: "The services at first were plain and simple. They are not so now. We were never told that Mr Haslam was an Anglo-Catholic. If I had known, I should not have gone." Those who thought this way might well have discerned an acceleration in the rate of change in the year leading up to the opening of the permanent church, when articles in the parish magazine argued the case for beliefs and practices that the "plain man", brought up in what he thought was the proper Anglican and Protestant tradition, found novel and, probably, threateningly <u>Roman</u> Catholic. Explained and recommended were:

- March 1930: kneeling at the Incarnatus in the Creed
- August 1930: incense
- October 1930: genuflection.

Most controversial of all, the article "What's in a Name?" in November 1930 examined the titles "Holy Communion", "Eucharist" and "Mass" and concluded that "Mass" was the best name of all: "Hearing Mass ... is a good straightforward expression like going to church, and one which every Englishman should be able to use without feeling awkward." Unfortunately, most Englishmen knew with even less awkwardness that "Mass" was what Roman Catholics did; only thirty years earlier Parliament had discussed a Bill that would have made it illegal for clergymen to describe the Holy Communion service as "Mass".[1]

The list of fittings sought for the new church, published in October 1930 would have excited further alarm, for it included six (not two) altar candlesticks, an aumbry for reserving a portion of the bread and wine consecrated at a communion service and, most emotive of all, a thurible for burning incense and an incense boat.

---

a) "Mass" is not used in documents extant from this period, apart from the one cited later.

This conflict over churchmanship, the "misunderstandings and grave allegations" noted by Richardson,[2] came to a head in the last weeks of 1930, just before the move to the permanent church. It coincided with Fr Haslam's decision to dispense with the unpaid services of the first organist, and the supporters of the deposed organist combined their protests on his behalf with objections to the supposed change from simple services to Anglo-Catholic ones.

Fr Haslam had encountered such arguments twice before he arrived in Long Thornton: his father had been assistant in 1896 to the Vicar of Christ Church, Sutton, who was then greatly unpopular with a section of his congregation for things "that have now become orthodox".[3] At St Anne, Wandsworth, where Fr Haslam was a curate in 1920–1, the Vicar had made changes to the conduct of services and felt bound to issue a "straightforward statement" in his church magazine that Fr Haslam repeated almost word for word when dealing in his turn with objectors to the pattern of worship that he was establishing at St Olave's: "Our sound endeavour has been to make St. Anne's a place of sound Anglo-Catholic worship with a great amount of tenderness and courtesy for some of her most faithful people who have been brought up under different ideas and methods of thought. We cannot please all, but we may save some."[4]

Mrs Bulbeck, an active member of the church from its beginning, countered the accusations thus: "We could not have everything straight away in a small building like the church hall. Mr Haslam never made any secret of his Anglo-Catholicism. It was obvious." Mrs Smith told the *News*: "It was always plain that he was an Anglo-Catholic. I welcome the changes. They have come about in a natural way." Fr Haslam had indeed said clearly in his first message to the parish in January 1928 that, since there were no pre-existing traditions, he proposed to introduce the type of service to which he had been accustomed: services would be like those held in Southwark Cathedral.[b] He proposed to meet the needs of those who wanted a simpler type of service by holding a fortnightly plain celebration of Holy Communion. However, no more than twelve people attended any one of these services, so they were discontinued.

In October 1928, after ten months in Long Thornton, Fr Haslam wrote that some good church people might "even find it impossible to adapt themselves" to what went on at St Olave's. In response to a request from some of the congregation, he wrote in June 1929 an article

---

b) To a well-informed Low Anglican, this would not have been encouraging. The Bishop wore cope and mitre in the cathedral, and in 1934 the MP for Devizes wrote to the Archbishop of Canterbury to complain about "posturings at the altar" and compared the cathedral with the [Roman Catholic] Brompton Oratory.[9]

on ceremonial, the "good manners that are used in the worship and service of God". In October 1929 the *Advertiser* quoted from the parish magazine: "My endeavour has been to make St. Olave's a place of sound Anglo-Catholic worship."[5] It is hard to understand how anyone, a further year on, could say "we did not realise that he was an Anglo-Catholic" and claim to have been misled.

In response to questions from the *News*, Fr Haslam replied forthrightly that services "have never been 'plain services for the plain man' and I never promised they would be." Objections met with a sharp reply in *St Olave's News* of July 1930: "If people who criticise religious customs which they do not understand, and have never been accustomed to, were to examine the authority for such customs, they would be astonished to discover that it is the Protestant, not the Catholic, who has been disloyal, not to say disobedient, to the 1662 Prayer Book."

Directly or indirectly, the Bishop was informed; he investigated and cited the disapproval of the Trustees of St Olave, Southwark, with whose money the Long Thornton church had largely been financed. Fr Haslam promised not to use incense or more than two candlesticks on the altar in the new church,[c] and not to use the term "Mass";[d] Evensong would be plain and simple, except for festival processions. Fr Haslam paid in person for ornaments purchased that could not now be used to be returned to the manufacturers. Incense eventually appeared in 1936.[e]

People were said to be leaving, and some no doubt did, but numbers of communicants rose during 1930, whilst departures were balanced by people coming from Streatham Vale, where the new church was certainly not Anglo-Catholic. The Bishop of Southwark was satisfied that the needs of the district were being met through the existence of these two churches of differing tradition.[6] At the Annual Meeting in 1931 Fr Haslam reported that attendances at the 11 a.m. service, at which ritual and music were most evident, had doubled.

None of the disputants at the time seems to have been troubled by what now seems an obvious point: from the first day of worship in the temporary church the main service of Sunday was a sung Holy Communion; never was Morning Prayer, or Mattins, offered to the parish as the focus of Sunday worship, though that was certainly still

---

c) Perhaps he was lucky not to suffer stronger censure: in 1924, in Ewell, a consistory court was convened because of objections to two candlesticks put on the altar by a "Romanist" vicar.[10]

d) By 1945 "Mass" was the publicly used term.

e) Bishop Garbett did not, however, object on principle to the use of incense within his diocese.[11]

"the main morning service of the Church of England".[7] A Commission of Enquiry set up during the First World War admitted that "church-going has largely come to mean attendance at such services as Mattins and Evensong, and the Holy Communion has been driven into the position of an exceptional service."[8] An Anglo-Catholic slogan ran "It is the Mass that matters", and Fr Haslam was clearly, we might now think, setting out his divergence from the middle-of-the-road norm of the day.

The ritual dispute might have occurred in any case—there had been complaints within the Church Council about non-consultation by the Vicar over changes to Evening Prayer—but it attracted greater local publicity through its association with the more dramatic 'Vicar sacks organist' story.[f] Perhaps Fr Haslam was over-certain that, with the new and wonderful building nearing completion, he could have all that he thought an Anglo-Catholic church should have. Once the Annual Meeting in April 1931 had passed a vote of confidence, he "confessed that he had had more difficulties at St Olave's than he had ever had in his life before, but in spite of all the difficulties he had never been so happy anywhere else."

And thus the "ritual problem at St Olave's [was] happily settled". The "misunderstandings and grave allegations", though, did not immediately die away: a year later the Annual Meeting heard that attendances at Evening Prayer were not growing very much, probably because of a "suspicion with regard to our church".[g] Nevertheless, the *News* thought that the church would "advance calmly as an Anglo-Catholic centre". The advance indeed happened, but it was not entirely calm.

---

f) See Chapter 19.

g) The Priest-in-Charge of The Ascension also had to tackle gossip in 1938 about being High.[12]

8: THE CHURCH OF BLUE COLUMNS

In one paragraph of the *St Olave's News* of February 1929 Fr Haslam recorded the Dedication of the mission church and the generosity of the Diocese of Southwark in establishing it; in the next he announced the "great task" of building a permanent church. Schemes for raising money were to start straight away, since the more the parishioners raised, the bigger the grants that could later be attracted. The area needed a social centre, and dual use of the mission church/hall was not really satisfactory. Thirdly, there was the need for the "spirit and atmosphere of reverence and devotion" that could only be found in a permanent church: "A beautiful church is the greatest aid we can have to the devotions of the worshippers. Beautiful things seen bring beautiful thoughts to the mind, and beautiful thoughts inspire beautiful words and deeds, which in turn result in beautiful lives."[a] Remarkable efforts were indeed made by local people to pay their part of the building costs, so that within two years the church was built, albeit in a form smaller than that once envisaged. Delays, of course, occurred, and by February 1930 even Fr Haslam was admitting to weariness with the process. Once the building was authorised and the contracts let, it was completed in well under a year.

The Ecclesiastical Commissioners began in March 1929 the legal processes necessary to establish a new District that could be endowed with funds to pay the Vicar's stipend. The Vicar of St Mark's, Mitcham, from whose parish the new District was to be formed, was pleased to agree with the proposals, no doubt happy to be relieved of some of his large and populous parish, and the Church Council of St Olave's accepted the stipulation that it must guarantee £100 per year towards the Vicar's stipend before making formal application to become a legally constituted Parish, rather than a Missionary District with no autonomy. The South London Church Fund quickly accepted responsibility for the stipend contribution. By Order in Council of 5 November 1929 the King both authorised the creation of this newly defined portion of the Church of England, and the building of a parish church, to be erected with the proceeds of the sale of the late church of St Olave, Southwark. The Crown was to be the patron of the parish, as stipulated in the Act of Parliament of 1918 that authorised the closure of the Southwark church.[1]

Because the new parish lay within the Deanery of Beddington, it came under the care of the Bishop of Woolwich, Rt Revd William Woodcock Hough, and it was he who visited the site in September 1928. A Building Committee was formed in May 1929; this was normal

---

a) This sounds like a quotation, but probably derives from Plato, *The Republic* 401, which may well have been part of Fr Haslam's education. Wordsworth in "Tintern Abbey" has similar ideas on the beneficent power of natural beauty.

practice in the planning of the Twenty-five churches in Southwark, so that local opinion and a wider knowledge of finance and administration could mix and be heard.

On 11 June the Bishop and Fr Haslam called on an architect, Arthur Campbell Martin,[b] at his office in Lincoln's Inn. At this first meeting Martin, as he recalled, suggested a church in Byzantine style. This, he thought, would express the aspirations of the parish as presented to him.[2] The Bishop of Woolwich commended the scheme to the committee, and the wrestling with size, cost and details began. It says much for both Martin and for the Building Committee that such an unconventional design was accepted without initial recorded objections.

Although Martin had no record of parish church work, he was chosen on account of his good work at the Royal Military Academy, Sandhurst, where he had been the architect for the enlargement of the chapel as a War Memorial, "in the Byzantine style of Northern Italy",[3] and at the hostel for Theology students of King's College, London, in Vincent Square, Westminster.

At Westminster Martin had been initially commissioned to complete the hostel already built to his design before the First World War. However, the Hostel Committee made changes in the layout that it wanted, and these led Martin to change the architectural style for the ground-floor chapel. Only fifteen feet in height and able to accommodate about a hundred people, the chapel's three bays and semicircular apse formed a plain Byzantine interior, composed of concrete vaulting springing from green marble columns.[c] Similarities with the chancel of St Olave's are obvious.

The question "Why was A. C. Martin selected?" cannot be answered with documentary certainty; reports of the Vincent Square chapel appeared in the press after that first meeting in Martin's office. It seems more likely that the idea came from the Bishop of Woolwich, than from the Priest-in-Charge, Fr Haslam; the Bishop was known to be businesslike and well informed, and he gave assistance to many parishes in matters of building alterations.[4] It is just possible that the Bishop of Southwark himself had some influence: he was certainly on the Council of the Theological Faculty at King's College, London, as was his successor, and on the Theological Committee from March 1930, though he was not present at the meetings when decisions about the new chapel were made.[5] Nevertheless, he clearly liked Martin's plans for St Olave's and later intervened to secure extra funding. Some years later he wrote of the Twenty-five that "we did our best to get really good architects, instead of turning to firms that produced convention [sic]

———————————

b) See Appendix D.

c) *The Builder*, 01/30, printed an illustration of the interior.

schemes from pigeon holes."[6] A study of Richardson's book shows how far this aim was realised.

Martin proposed a church in Byzantine style, built of concrete clad in brick. The plan was in the form of a nave with two shallow transepts, a chancel and a rectangular apse at the East end, with a tower and entrance at the West end. The chancel, nave and transepts met under a dome at the crossing, with the vestries on the South side of the chancel, and a Lady Chapel on the North side. [These compass points are liturgical, not geographical, ones: the building is not aligned on an east-west axis, as is often the case—to have put it so would have made it crooked on the available site.]

Given that the foundation of finance was a probable £7,000 from the Tooley Street site, it is a little surprising that the initial plans were costed at £17,000. At its first consideration of the plans in July 1928 the Church Council decided to build only a portion of the church, though still for about 440–500 people, leaving the Lady Chapel, the second bay of the nave and the West tower to follow at a later date. More contentious was Mr Field's objection to the "arched" ["flat"?] roof. He recommended a timbered ridge roof, a proposal that the Council adopted. After discussion of the exterior of the truncated building, the Council recommended that it be "made more beautiful"; already the Council understood that the complete church might not be seen, at least by the first generation of parishioners.

New plans, with a pointed roof, were presented to the Building Committee on 1 October, and went on open display, accompanied by a scale model, two days later at a social evening in the Meopham Road Welfare Hall. Then it was the turn of two central committees to view the plans: the Twenty-five Churches Fund Committee and the Central Advisory Board in Southwark both rejected the pointed roof, on grounds of cost (the architect confirmed that it would be dearer than the flat roof) and of appearance; it would spoil a "very beautiful and most imposing design". Although the views of the local Building Committee had, according to Fr Haslam, been "treated with careful consideration", Mr Field claimed at a Church Council meeting that the Vicar had been disloyal to the Building Committee, an accusation that generated much discussion. He proposed a motion of protest, which was lost by nine votes to five, and he resigned from the Council.[d] After this interlude the architect had to produce plans of the reduced-size church with a flat roof, which were approved in December.

A funding gap of £2,100 at the beginning of 1930 nearly caused the postponement of the project for another year; even the smaller version of the church seemed to be out of reach. Seven firms had tendered for the building contract, but the cost, including the architect's fees of £680,

---

d) Ten years later, when Mayor, he contributed to the New Altar fund.

31

was about £14,000. Martin was able in January to suggest economies[e] that would reduce the cost to about £11,000, and these cuts were accepted by the Building Committee, but with a plea that the sanctuary space should not be reduced, even though around £500 would thereby be saved. After these reductions in expense, the plans went to the Ecclesiastical Commissioners, who approved them on 3 February.

Meanwhile, General Cuthbertson conveyed the news of the enforced reductions to Bishop Garbett, who undertook to argue for more grants. To the City Parochial Charities Fund he wrote: "I feel we ought to build a good church in the place of the old St. Olave's, and I do not want to interfere unnecessarily with excellent plans." The Fund granted £500, as did the Twenty-five Churches Fund. Even before the grants were announced Fr Haslam had been told that about £12,500 could be spent, but £1,000, beyond what had already been collected, would have to be raised locally. He was confident that a deficit could be covered by local giving; £400 had been raised within a year, and he cited the example of his previous parish, "in one of the most poverty-stricken districts in South London", where £2,000 had been raised for repairs. The Twenty-five Churches Fund grant meant that contracts could be let, and Hall, Beddall & Co.[f] of Pitfield Wharf, London, began work on 6 March 1930 immediately after the Urban District Council had given its permission.

In addition to the building there was still a pipe organ to be found and paid for, probably by loan and repayment in instalments. The Church Council had delegated the task of procurement to Fr Haslam and Canon Gale of Sutton: they located an instrument owned by the firm of Rest Cartwright that had been built for a country mansion at a pre-1914 cost of around £2,000. Although this instrument had probably been in mind since February, there was a second consultation, about an organ from the firm of Brindley and Foster, but by November the organ from Rest Cartwright & Co.[g] had been purchased for £750, plus £120 for the console and an electric blower.

Costs and the estimated debt rose: the builders' tender of £11,287 was exceeded by £600, partly because of extra foundation and drainage works, whilst the expected debt (including the organ) became £1,300,

---

e) It is not clear what these were, though Martin wrote in *Souvenir* that the porches were temporary.

f) This firm also tendered in 1927 for Martin's work at King's, London, but their price was some £580 higher than the lowest one. There is no record of who else tendered for the contract at St Olave's.

g) See Appendix E.

then £1,500, by March 1931. The inclusive cost of building and fittings was later reported as £14,000.[h]

May was the month for laying the foundation stone. It had been hoped that the recently retired Archbishop of Canterbury would perform this office, but by May he was terminally ill. His place was taken, perhaps less prestigiously, by Bishop Garbett's mother, "a venerable old lady" (so described by the *News*) who had performed such ceremonies at other new churches in Southwark. The service on the afternoon of 3 May was necessarily an open-air one, but fortunately the morning rain relented until the service was over, though the Bishop's address had to be curtailed to escape a thunderstorm. The architect presented Mrs Garbett with a silver trowel,[i] inscribed "3rd May 1930. St. Olave's Church, Norbury. Foundation Stone"; she laid the stone with these words: "In the faith of Jesus Christ, we place this stone in the name of God the Father, God the Son, and God the Holy Ghost. Amen." The Bishop appealed to those present to bring others into the fellowship of the church before the new building was opened and hoped that the new church would be remarkable in many ways among the new churches in Southwark. The stone itself, now hard to view because of the garages later built alongside, has a cross in the middle, "*Laus Deo*" [Praise to God] above and "May 1930" below. As a token of the church's link with its diocese, a piece of stone from Southwark Cathedral was provided, to be built into the wall.

In early June building was going ahead at a rapid pace, and continued through the heat wave of August until the outside was finished in early October. Meanwhile, Mr Lewis and Mr Woolven, two members of the congregation, had been making an oak altar, for which a Roman altar stone, including a relic, was given by Mr J. Kemp, one of the stonemasons who lived next to the cemetery, and who was among the first persons to be confirmed at St Olave's. A list published in October of desirable fittings, worth sixty pounds, brought a ready response, though not all the donations could be used, because of objections voiced to the use of incense. Some brass ornaments deemed unsuitable for the new church were sent to British Guiana. The pewter almsdishes from St Olave, Southwark, were available, though the silver-gilt flagon, communion cup and plate from there, nominally valued at £300, only arrived in mid-1931. Also from the Trustees of St Olave,

---

h) According to Richardson, Cachemaille-Day's notable church of St Saviour, New Eltham, also of reinforced concrete and brick, cost £11,000. At Mitcham the concrete work was more complex, and the foundations in the clay soil were expensive.

i) The trowel was presented to Fr Haslam and remains in the possession of the church.

Southwark, came the pulpit, already in the mission church, though not yet attached to its steps, the font, to be placed in the North transept, the tenor bell and the older clock bell. Oak choir stalls were purchased for £10 10s., a twentieth of their value, through the good offices of the Priest-in-Charge of the Good Shepherd church at Carshalton Beeches.j

The whole floor area, apart from essential gangways and a space by the font, was filled with chairs, 367 in the Nave alone. To reach the target of 515 (including choir) sittings, the architect measured the spaces extraordinarily carefully: 20 in. per person and rows 2 ft 10¾ in. deep. Ten years later many of the chairs had gone and the transepts were differently used.

Apart from the flooring, laid by Italian workmen, and decoration, the church was ready for formal inspection by 15 December. Thornsome of the *News* took a look: "The blue pillars, the red tiles before the altar and the Byzantine dome—I love them." Caröe and Passmore on behalf of the Ecclesiastical Commissioners inspected it on 16 January 1931 and certified it as well built and fit to become a parish church, though they made some recommendations to the architect for small modifications, just in time for the consecration next day by the Lord Bishop of Southwark.

j) Caröe and Passmore in *EC* 91151/1 state that the choir seating came from St Olave, Southwark; this is not obvious from the pictures of that church and is not what appears in *Minutes* or *Inventory*.

9: SET APART FOR WORSHIP

The local newspapers are clear that 500–600 people were present on the afternoon of 17 January 1931 for the Consecration, and that the 515 seats provided were not enough. People at the front of the transepts can have had only a partial, or else an uncomfortable, view of proceedings. Now that the architecture is no longer novel and the decoration is plainer than that which greeted the first congregation, we are fortunate that the reporter for the *News* had a sympathetic eye and a rich verbal palette from which to describe the building in its newness. The half-tone illustration in the paper is drab, compared with the words that bring to life the wonder of the place and of the occasion:

Picture a church like no other in Christendom, the Church of St. Olave, Long Thornton, as it stood on Saturday afternoon for its consecration, before three bishops.

Outside, terraced in oriental towers of comforting brown-red brick, it is low, square-lined, flat-topped. Inside, new-built, it is tunnelled, domed, and shaded, cleanly as though compass and pencil have swung swift curves. Smooth blue columns arise in concrete, their capitals fashioned with gold and blue-leaf twinings, shallow as Devon rose-baskets. Crimson cords, streaking from vaulted arches, support bell-like lampshades burnished in dark metal.

Groins and arches are edged in pale primrose; eyes are uplifted by stabbing poles of red. A carpet flows scarlet from a southern porch, wrinkles past blue altar rails up two short steps, till it rests at last before the altar, fresh yellow carpentered by St. Olave's churchmen.

Above the altar, misted with bright distance, though one hundred feet only from the southern door, is stretched a square of purple cloth glowing with imperial dye. Grey velvet hangs against an eastern door, while from western windows fall pure shafts of light. Twin bowls of darkness mark the veteran oak of old St Olave's, Southwark, font and pulpit. Save for the hard, round shine of the electric bulbs, there is nothing that is not soft or rich or strange.

THE SERVICE BEGINS

The doors are locked and the church is filled with people waiting. A few moments ago they saw clergy and choir pass by to the church entrance. There was delay, then the crunch of steps, next the voice of the Bishop of Southwark crying: "I am ready to proceed to the Consecration."

Choir and clergy passed out with hymn books raised, latecomers slipped in, the keys were turned. Now began a period of waiting. Those inside had nought to do save stand and listen. Sometimes, as cold shivers crept along the wood-block floor, they stirred uneasily. Outside the wind never droned more sadly. None knew where the robed procession walked. But, borne on the wind, now strong and near, now faint and far, came voices: "O Lord," sang the voices; "O Lord, have mercy on us." Shifting from point to point, the singing continued for many minutes.

Suddenly the listeners started as thrice the door resounded to a blow. Outside the Bishop chanted, "Lift up your heads, O ye gates, and be ye lift up, ye everlasting doors: and the King of glory shall come in."

The doors were opened, the Bishop entered with his cross-bearer. Raising on high his silver-crooked pastoral staff, he invoked peace on the house, then entered farther and knelt at a small desk, or faldstool, in the centre aisle.

Behind him came the Bishops of Woolwich and Kingston ... A robe stiff with blue and gold brocade was laid about the Bishop of Southwark's shoulders as he rose from his devotions and led the procession to the chancel steps. All knelt. Children who had not found seats rested their knees before the Bishop's faldstool. Others bowed their heads within the cover of the porch. The aisles were full with kneeling worshippers.

THE CONSECRATION

It was a moment of mystery, of whispering humility. The Bishop placed the keys of the church upon the altar, then desired the people to keep silence for a space.

After this—the people followed the directions in the consecration service—*the Bishop, attended by his chaplains and the Incumbent, and bearing his staff in his hand, shall proceed to the Font for the blessing thereof, a psalm to be sung meanwhile. With his attendants he shall return to the chancel. Then shall the Bishop, standing at the Table to be hallowed, turn himself to the people and say, "The Lord be with you." Then shall he turn towards the Table and lay his hand upon the Table. Then shall the Table be covered with the fair linen cloth; and the ornaments, vessels, and their cloths shall be presented to the Bishop, who shall place them thereon.*

When these things were done, the bewigged Chancellor read the Sentence of Consecration. The Sentence of Consecration then being laid upon the Table, the Bishop signed it.

Turning then to the people the Bishop thrice opened and closed his arms invitingly, not moving his elbows from his hips the while. Holding aloft his staff in his right hand, he said: "We set apart from all common or profane uses this house and whatsoever therein is consecrated, and dedicate the same for the mysteries of the Church."

"Good people," he went on, "I have now signed the Sentence of Consecration of this church; and declare it to be dedicated henceforth to the glory of God, under the title of St. Olave's, Mitcham; and I direct that the Document be enrolled and preserved in the muniments of the Registry of this Diocese."

In his sermon, Dr Garbett noted that St Olave's was the thirteenth church to be built or enlarged in connection with the Twenty-five Churches Fund. The old St. Olave's had, at the time of its demolition, nothing of interest except its name. It was not interesting historically, it was not interesting artistically, nor was it of any practical value. When a church lacked historical association, beauty, architectural interest or practical use, it was far better that it should be demolished and the money used for building churches in the districts which required them.

The church, he pointed out, was set apart for worship. Worship was almost a universal instinct of the human heart. Dr. Garbett then delivered a "brilliant discourse" on the nature of worship and religion. He "ranged over all the centuries, culling instances and illustrations from every culture and clime."

The Bishop also reminded the church congregation of its responsibilities: "Worship may be offered by glorious ceremonial in a wonderful cathedral, or it may be without any kind of ceremonial in a whitewashed chapel. And the worship in neither case will count as anything unless behind it is the spirit of devoted love. Your worship, however beautiful it may be, counts as nothing in the sight of Almighty God unless it is the worship of love.

"As century follows century, may this church be a living centre. You must be missionaries building up the work of the church, inviting others to come, so that the church may be a great hope and influence for good in this place."

Once the visitors had left, the life of worship in the new church began on the Sunday morning, when the Bishop of Southwark celebrated Holy Communion and was impressed to find one hundred and sixty communicants there. At the 11 a.m. Sung Eucharist the preacher was the Rector of Sutton, who noted "spirit and enthusiasm and real happiness". And so the "strikingly beautiful" church as visitors saw it, built in less than eleven months, rose above the red-tiled terraces of Long Thornton, a house of God where only a few years earlier all had been fields and mud.

10: A STRIKING EXAMPLE

"The best modern churches are those which unite modern design and construction with a sense of tradition." So wrote Fr Gabriel Hebert in 1935.[1] After eighty years it is easy to forget that St Olave's was once new and the subject of illustration and description in the church and architectural press. In 1933 *The Guardian*[a] published a picture of the interior and commented: "A striking example of modern church architecture. Byzantine in feeling, it depends for its beauty upon an impression of breadth and spaciousness, obtained by the original treatment of the arches and vaults."[2] In the *Journal of the Royal Institute of British Architects*, Nugent Cachemaille-Day included a picture of a barely finished St Olave's in his article "Ecclesiastical Architecture in the Present Age", though he made no mention of the church in the text of the article.[3]

Arthur Martin himself described the exterior as "simple—some may regard it as severe", and from the interior he singled out the qualities of light—"the church is light, and the altar, domes and piers are all somewhat mysteriously bright beyond one's expectations"—and its spaciousness: "Largeness is always comparative, but spaciousness is not. It is a quality that a building either has or has not got, and is independent of its size. This spaciousness St. Olave's surely has." Dr Garbett thought it "spacious, striking, and dignified".[4]

Some seventy years on, Kenneth Richardson saw St Olave's, on historical and architectural grounds, as "undoubtedly one of the most rewarding of the Southwark 'Twenty-five' ".[5] He noted the "long and squat" profile of the "austere" exterior and the details, such as the round-headed windows and the embossed rainwater hoppers.[b] In 2003 the inspecting architect, while recording the many items outside in need of repair, also described the aesthetic qualities inside:

One of the great joys and surprises of St Olave's is the interior. The unfinished exterior does not prepare one for the fine architectural volumes that have been achieved inside. ... It is the domed ceiling over the crossing which allows the light from the transepts to enter to the centre of church and gives a real focus to the building. ... The interior of the church is finished largely with painted plaster below vaulted ceilings with windows often set behind an inner arched opening in the form of a mock triforium. This works very successfully architecturally, giving depth and scale to the building.[6]

To these professional comments can be added the many expressions of surprise and pleasure made over the years by contractors working on

---

a) A church periodical, not today's daily newspaper.

b) See Illustration 17.

site, polling station staff and all kinds of visitor; the interior speaks through its calm and spaciousness. Those who do not frequent churches can see that it is not of the type normally shown in period drama on television; indeed, it is still discernibly modern, or at least not old-fashioned.

The word "Byzantine", so freely applied to St Olave's, deserves some explanation and clarification. The term has its origins in the eastern Roman empire, ruled from Constantinople [modern Istanbul] which itself grew out of the earlier Byzantium; Justinian, Emperor from 527 to 565, ordered a huge building programme that included the multiple-domed Hagia Sophia in Constantinople and churches in Ravenna, in northern Italy, a town intended to be the new capital of his empire in Italy. Two of these Ravenna buildings, which were more accessible than Constantinople to English visitors, illustrate and complicate the ideas contained in "Byzantine". San Vitale is octagonal in plan with a central dome and a semicircular apse; San Appolinare Novo has the plan of a Roman basilica: a wide nave, flanked by round-arched colonnades, leads to a semicircular apse. Both have plain exteriors in brick; the windows are round-headed; the interiors are richly decorated in mosaic. Thus "Byzantine" includes elements of plan, constructional features and decoration.[7]

For about thirty years from the last years of the nineteenth century neo-Byzantine became a style used in English church architecture. The most prominent church building that uses the Byzantine elements of domes, arches and decoration is Westminster Cathedral (1895–1903). Elsewhere in London, Christchurch, Brixton Road, (1899–1902) has a large, undecorated, dome to allow a large congregation an uninterrupted view of the pulpit; St Peter, Acton Green, (1915) and St Augustine, Belvedere, (1916) both adopt the basilica plan and the constructional features, but not the decoration.[8]

At St Olave's, according to Martin, "the underlying 'motif' is Byzantine, yet the treatment of the domes and arches are unlike any individual church of that date." Whereas medieval churches, with their narrowness and height, "radiated both mystery and emotion in a ... superstitious age," his design aimed at the "breadth of outlook so characteristic of individual intelligence today that accepts the help of Science."[c] There is no decoration, no semi-darkness, but a lot of light; Martin knew this and invited us to "notice the wonderful graduations of shading and reflected light revealed on the curving surfaces."

"Byzantine" in St Olave's applies to style rather than plan: the dome, the round-headed arches and the arcades, all severely undecorated, constitute the style, but in plan the church is in fact a Gothic one,

---

c) He said of his work at Sandhurst that the chapel was to be "beautiful in a spiritual sense, not too obviously 'religious' ".[19]

contrary to Martin's claim that the building is "a reversion in plan to the very early churches of Asia Minor". The plan of typical early Byzantine churches is a Greek cross, ✚, or a square, and the basilica plan is a rectangle with an apse at the East end, but Martin's original proposal, including a second bay in the nave, used the Latin cross plan, ➕, familiar from our medieval cathedrals. The chancel was divided from the nave by a low wall, and the form of worship required that the focus should be on the altar at the East end of the building. The incomplete nave and the re-ordering of the interior with a nearly central altar have in fact made the building more Byzantine in plan than first intended.

At St Olave's an ancient tradition was re-created by modern materials and construction, as the architect explained: "The roof and all the vaulting is of the most recent type of reinforced concrete. In this respect at least the church is very modern. But the old builders would have used it had it been available, and if the great church of St. Sophia at Constantinople had had its dome reinforced it would not have given the anxiety it has." Reinforced concrete, the subject of several articles in *The Builder* in the mid-1920s, was a nearly novel material for church use,[d] even though Martin had used it in 1920–1 for vaults and a dome at Sandhurst, and the ICBS wanted more information about it before discussing the making of grants, since the stability of the building depended on it. The Trussed Concrete Steel Co. Ltd, or Truscon,[e] supplied the reinforced concrete,[9] as it had for Martin's work at Sandhurst and at Vincent Square. The biggest casting in St Olave's is the central dome, 41 ft in diameter and 33 ft in internal height; forces exerted by this dome are contained by a rolled steel channel ring beam which is in turn supported by four channels, one across each corner of the square.[10] The weight is borne by the brick walls and the eight concrete columns.

The flat roofing, the subject of earlier controversy, was covered with Macasfelt, "a comparatively modern material", whose makers claimed that its composition of layers of bitumen and waterproofed sheeting, surfaced with fine macadam, made it superior to asphalt, since it would not crack.[11] By early 1939 the roof was leaking, and more modern materials have not usually lasted for longer than fifteen years at a time.

Because of the concrete base of the building there was no possibility of using underfloor hot-water piping for radiators, so a McLary pipeless system was installed (a similar one went into The Holy Redeemer

---

d) *The Builder* in 1926 illustrated the 1915 church of St Peter, Acton Green, which used reinforced concrete.

e) Truscon, founded in the UK in 1907, from American parents, was the leading contractor in this material. It was involved in the design of the enormous dome of the Melbourne Public Library, illustrated in *The Builder* 08/08/13. This might have put the possibility of concrete vaults and domes into Martin's mind.

church).[12] The system had admirers and satisfied users; the Vicar of Holy Trinity, Lambeth, recommended it on the grounds of "economy, cleanliness, freedom from smells and, above all, efficiency". [13] Heat from a furnace in a heating chamber beneath the vestries went directly into the church through an opening in the wall of the South transept. The installation had caused problems even before the consecration: Caröe and Passmore found cracked plaster on the wall next to the furnace flue, to be remedied by the introduction of fireclay flue pipes, and required large gratings to be fitted in the outside wall of the heating chamber, because of the danger from coke fumes. Converted to oil-burning, the system survived into the early 1970s, but by then was "officially condemned as both a fire and noxious fumes risk".[14]

Even the foundations of the building, in clay soil, presented constructional challenges. The architect said that he had rarely seen ground in a more sticky condition (the Archdeacon's car got stuck in the mud during an early visit to the site)[15] and initially thought of foundations a minimum of 4½ ft deep, but specified ones between five and eight feet deep below ground level. A heavy bed of concrete supported the brick walls, generally 2 ft 3 in. thick. 380,000 bricks were used, with 2 in. rustic red ones as the facing.[16]

Not surprisingly, in an unconventional building, some faults appeared soon after completion: chalk stains from damp appeared in the outer walls, and the paint on the blue columns peeled because of acid in the cement core. Serious cracks in the ceiling and arches were repaired during 1935–6 and have reappeared since, especially in the arches between the transepts and the dome area. Specialist professional examination has assessed the movement, between reinforced concrete and brick sections of the building, as not of structural significance.[17] Acoustically, the building perhaps left something to be desired, at least in the days before sound support systems; Thornvale complained of a "rumbling echo" from the preacher at a Guides' District Parade in 1933. Martin's later Byzantine building at St Luke, Camberwell, may have had similar problems.[18]

To those who saw the church in its first few weeks, the pillars supporting the dome were the "only note of colour ... pale blue with a touch of gold". By October 1931 the columns had been repainted in different shades of blue. The walls and ceilings were left as bare plaster and not painted until 1936, when flat cream paint was applied and the redecoration "revealed the dignity of the architecture". The blue columns, though not the capitals, then lost their colour until the 1950s.[f]

---

f) See Illustration 14.

11: RESERVATION, OUR LADY AND INCENSE

Once the new church was open, the articles on Anglo-Catholic beliefs and practices continued:

- September 1931: Fasting Communion
- September 1931: The Sign of the Cross
- April 1932: Vestments
- June 1932: Reservation
- March 1933: Reservation
- November 1935: Incense
- December 1935: Fasting
- November 1936: Prayers for the departed.

Reservation of the Sacrament began without any controversy, not least because Fr Haslam made a reasoned case for its utility in ministry to the sick and did not adopt 'advanced' services such as Benediction. Incense and a statue of Our Lady caused rather more trouble.

In June 1932 Fr Haslam introduced Reservation thus: "To reserve the Blessed Sacrament means to keep a portion of what has been consecrated after the service is over. ... The place of reservation is usually a small safe which is called an aumbry, which is built into the north wall of the sanctuary. A lamp with a white light is kept burning in the sanctuary of churches in which the Holy Sacrament is reserved. ... There are sick people who cannot come to church at all, and to whom the reserved Sacrament can be taken." By September 1932 application had been made to the Bishop for permission, and the practice began in early 1933; at Easter 1933 twenty-one people unable to attend church received communion through the use of the reserved sacrament. A second article announced that "there is now a white light always burning" and encouraged a response on entering or leaving the building: "Do not let us hesitate if some instinct or feeling prompts us to make some outward act of reverence." Genuflection might be implied, but the time was not right for the teaching of such a gesture.

The practice of reservation had became much more widespread during and after the war, because of an increased need for the giving of Holy Communion at short notice and because large numbers of people during the war desired to pray before the reserved sacrament.[1] Dr Garbett addressed the Clergy Synod of his diocese on reservation; he spoke of authority and legality, but also showed a sensitivity not always attributed to him. He recognised that the practice was of great antiquity in the Church elsewhere in Europe and allowed the strong pastoral need in industrial society for access by the sick to the sacrament; he accepted the private freedom to say prayers near the place where the sacrament was kept. Although he himself had experienced the "emotional appeal" of public services of adoration, such as Benediction, when travelling in Catholic Europe, he did not think that in the Church of England there was a justification for a form of public worship that was of only mediaeval origin and was neither grounded in the New Testament nor practised in the Orthodox churches.[2]

Fr Haslam would presumably have attended this 1925 Synod and can have had no doubt about the rules in the Southwark Diocese. Unlike many Anglo-Catholic clergy, he did not despise the new Prayer Book,[g] but his assent to the rules of 1928 was neither complete nor unambiguous, as may be inferred from his encouragement, mentioned earlier, of an "outward act of reverence", even though "ceremony" was forbidden. His introductory article of 1932 added to the sick those "prevented by the conditions of their work from attending [Mass] in church" as beneficiaries of reservation: "They can come to church for a few minutes, in intervals of their work, subject to some simple rule of fasting, kneel down and receive the Blessed Sacrament, say a word of thanksgiving, and go back to their work, strengthened by the Bread of Life." This idea was in accordance with Anglo-Catholic thought of the time,[h] but contrary to the 1928 rules. It is impossible to tell whether Fr Haslam actually used the reserved sacrament in this way.

In March 1935 the Church Council discussed an offer to give to the church a statue of the Blessed Virgin Mary. The offer came from the St Olave's branch of the Mothers' Union, eighty in number, whose banner had recently been placed in the church; according to Mrs Bulbeck, the Enrolling Member, three members had made gifts to purchase the figure. Fr Haslam asked that there should be a frank discussion and said that he would not allow an application for a Faculty to proceed if any one member dissented; the Council agreed unanimously to go ahead. After the Council's decision, the Mothers' Union purchased the statue, but three families, and Fr Haslam thought they were representative of many more, raised objections; postponement was unavoidable if there was not to be friction among church members. He admitted that the matter had been "rushed through" the Council, and it seems surprising, in view of the unhappiness of late 1930, that greater care was not taken over sounding out opinions <u>before</u> announcing a decision on something inevitably contentious.

Fr Haslam realised that there was an "urgent need for instruction and frank discussion", held individual discussions with doubters and

---

g) See start of Chapter 6.

h) See, for example, the contribution by Fr Darwell Stone in *Papers of the Anglo-Catholic Congress*, 1923.

wrote a long article in the April Magazine about the place of Mary in Catholic Christianity:

She alone both saw Him born and saw Him die: she alone heard both His first infant cry and His last commendation of His soul into His Father's keeping. ... To Him we give the worship and adoration which are due to God, and to God alone: to her we give only that which may rightly be given to a creature, profoundest reverence and homage.

Elsewhere, his public instructional tone, heard at a distance in time, can seem slightly condescending:

I am firmly convinced that much of the prejudice and dislike which exists in the minds of many earnest Christians today in regard to some Church customs and practices is due to a widespread as well as profound ignorance both of their origin and what they really mean.

The postponement was reported in the local press in May. At the end of the month the Council heard a talk on "The Authority and Use of Statues in Churches", and in June Fr Haslam told the Council that "feeling" had been overcome. The statue was blessed on 8 September 1935, the Feast of the Nativity of the Blessed Virgin Mary, a Marian day retained in the calendar of the Book of Common Prayer.

Some of the "feeling" was clearly hurtful: two days after the blessing Fr Haslam told the Mothers' Union that Mrs Bulbeck had resigned and was leaving the parish. She gave up church work on medical advice and sadly admitted that she had "spent other people's money" on a figure that they had hoped to put into church.

By September 1937 Fr Haslam was looking for a bigger and better statue. The three donors had by this time left the church, and the Mothers' Union agreed to pass the first statue[i] to a Fr Fowler.[3] At some point another statue was purchased, about two feet high, on a black base. The present statue,[j] blessed on 16 August 1942, was given in memory of the mother of Fr Keene, the priest who looked after the parish while Fr Haddelsey was in the Forces. The second statue found its way in 1943 to the church of All Saints, Buckie.[4]

In 1939–40 the North transept became a Lady Chapel: a new altar, blue-curtained in the English[k] style, to plans from Mowbrays of London, was set up on a platform adjacent to the temporary wall and the font

---

i) A photograph shows a plain white figure, about eighteen inches high.

j) Marketed as the "Murillo Madonna" by The Pax House of Westminster.

k) See Anson pp. 307–12.

took its present place at the West end of the nave. The altar was dedicated on 1 October 1940.

The use of incense, forbidden by Bishop Garbett in early 1931, was again under discussion in the summer of 1935: Fr Sibellas, the curate appointed to take charge of the new District of The Ascension, addressed a meeting of sixty parishioners on the subject, and in November the Church Council, presumably after informal discussions in the intervening months, agreed, by sixteen votes to five, to the use of incense at the 11 a.m. Sunday Eucharist. The Bishop of Southwark, now Dr Richard Parsons, was asked for approval, but declined because of the size of the minority.

Incense had come to be used more openly in the Church of England; a picture of the outdoor procession of clergy at the start of the 1920 Anglo-Catholic Congress shows a priest carrying a thurible.[5] After 1927–8 Bishops began to make their own local regulations on worship,[6] and it may be that concern over clergy overriding the wishes of parishioners played a part in both Bishops' decisions: it had become clear in the Parliamentary debates on the proposed Prayer Books of 1927–8 that there was "long-accumulating resentment against too many Anglo-Catholics"[7] for thrusting their way on their parishioners.

What happened next is not entirely clear, but from Easter Day 1936 incense <u>was</u> used; within the Church Council Fr Haslam stated that "the matter was not for discussion." He did not wilfully disobey his Bishop's instructions on any other matter; in his statement to the Council he sounds an exasperated man, a state of mind possibly created by the earlier discussions and delays over the statue of the Blessed Virgin Mary and by criticism of his strict policy on baptisms.[1]

---

1) See Chapter 18.

12: FASTING COMMUNION AND THE PEOPLE'S COMMUNION

The 1928 Prayer Book suggested that fasting before communion might be "used or not used, according to every man's conscience in the sight of God," a view repeated by the Archbishop of York in 1931. He could not see why people should be called on to "cut short their sleep on the morning of their rest", nor did he think it profitable for people to attend Holy Communion at 8 a.m. and then attend the same order of service later in the morning.[1] In the same year Revd L. S. Hunter argued that, by insisting on the rule of fasting, the Church was cutting off a large number of people who needed the sacrament and was giving others a feeling that they had done something wrong when they communicated after having a cup of tea.[2]

For Fr Haslam, though, a morning cup of tea broke the fast and should be resisted; he thought that observance of the rules brought more communicants. Fasting might well be open to individual conscience, but no provision was made at St Olave's for the general congregation to receive the sacrament at the Sung Eucharist, whatever conscience might have said. The infirm may or may not have been the only communicants at the Sung Eucharist: the Book of Common Prayer was clear that at least three persons should communicate, as well as the priest, so suitable persons who had sustained the fast until late morning were probably on hand to ensure some communion by lay people.

The drawbacks of this scheme of worship were increasingly pointed out after the First World War. A former army chaplain called in 1918 for the Holy Communion to be at a time suitable for all, not just the "officer class".[3] Other ex-chaplains were anxious to make the Communion service the "main, corporate, family congregational act of worship"[4] in the Church of England, an ideal that the two-congregation outcome, though not intention, of the Anglo-Catholic system could not deliver. Some priests in working-class areas began holding the Communion service at around 9.30 a.m. on Sundays, when people did not have to rise early for work, and could still fast before Mass.

Form and advocacy for this idea came in 1935 from Fr Gabriel Hebert in *Liturgy and Society*, where he argued against the old scheme, "the great blunder of the Anglo-Catholic movement": "However beautiful [the late-morning Sung Eucharist] may be, the people are spectators at the liturgy, and not in the full sense partakers in it." Without the communion of the people it was a "maimed rite".[5] The timetable in his solution was, however, still dictated by the demands of the fasting communion, which he commended: a Parish Communion at which all could receive the sacrament, with or without the music and ceremonial used at the sung service, could take place at 9 or 9.30 a.m., because the fast could thereby reasonably be maintained. Other practical, rationalising reasons followed: later rising for the one day of the week when people did not have to go to work (Saturday morning was part of working hours well into the 1950s); lunch could be prepared at an easier time, and families could attend one service together.

Some parishes had tried a parish communion, including Mitcham Parish Church, whose Vicar tried a 9.45 a.m. Sunday Holy Communion from January 1928, but it only happened once a month; the main service was still Morning Prayer. The introduction of such a service at St Olave's was an immediate aim of the new Vicar in 1938, conveyed to the Church Council within two months of his arrival. In preparatory articles in the parish magazine he cited Fr Hebert's work and argued that the existing system led to fewer regular communions. Most people, he claimed, did not attend both the early and the 11 a.m. services, and many only attended the chief "parish family" service in mid-morning and thus were not receiving the sacrament, so that a long-cherished aim of the Catholic revival—more frequent communions—was being thwarted. To those who only wanted a quiet early communion service, he said that it was a mistake to make Holy Communion no more than a set of personal devotions. Though he said, too, that fasting and prayer were still needed, Fr Haddelsey seems to have been less assertive about the virtues of the pre-communion fast.

The new service began in December 1938, and the Vicar called it "outstandingly successful" at the Annual Meeting in 1939. Communicant numbers ranged from fifteen to thirty. Fr Haddelsey nevertheless retained the sung 11 a.m. service and, by calling it "High Mass", seemed to underline its traditional Anglo-Catholic significance; he did not follow the logic of one pioneer of parish communion and run down the former main service in favour of the new. By the 1960s there was an early Holy Communion and a single Parish Communion at 9.30 a.m., by which time the fasting rules, after relaxation by Rome, no longer governed the pattern of services.

13: GOING TO CHURCH

With the aid of some guesswork as well as evidence, let us take ourselves to the main Sunday morning service in St Olave's in, say, 1933. Summoned by the tenor bell brought from St Olave, Southwark, we can approach the building across the grounds from Church Walk or from Middle Road. Chairs fill the central nave space, right up to the start of the raised chancel area, marked out by a low wall. In the transept to our left[a] there are more chairs, almost surrounding the font; in the transept to our right there are fewer chairs, for an altar[b] with posts and curtains in the English style has been set up for the daily services of Holy Communion. A purple curtain covers the far wall above the High Altar, for as yet there is no Christus Rex figure to attract our eyes. A white light tells us that the Blessed Sacrament is indeed reserved here for the sick and those who cannot attend the service. Some of the arriving worshippers bow or genuflect to honour the Sacrament, but many do not. Some three hundred or so people are here, children as well as adults; the Sunday Schools will assemble in the afternoon.

Eleven o'clock comes, and the choir of boys and men, wearing surplices, enters, preceded by a server wearing a cotta, who carries the processional cross. After the choir come more servers in cottas, some of whom carry lighted candles. The curate, Mr (not yet called Father) Davis, follows, and last comes the Vicar, wearing a chasuble whose colour matches that of the embroidered frontal cloth of the altar. The first hymn, from *The English Hymnal*, is sung. Afterwards all turn to the Book of Common Prayer from which the service is conducted, though some alertness and familiarity will be needed to skip the parts that are not customarily used and allow for additions; Fr Haslam begins with the Preparation, a Roman confessional rite for the priest and then, after the opening Lord's Prayer and Collect, the recitation of the Ten Commandments is omitted, its place taken by a Summary of the Law provided in the alternative order of service of 1928.

After more prayers, a portion of scripture from the New Testament is read by the curate from the Gothic-style, silver-plated lectern to our left, and then follows the second hymn, during which a procession of servers

a) At some point in the 1930s a children's corner was formed there.

b) The installation was organised in 1933 by Revd V. P. Davis, the first assistant curate, and paid for by an anonymous parishioner. The original posts were commendably plain—no plump *putti* until 1964. The altar, in oak, inset with a stone slab containing a relic plug with unknown contents, and with extensions at either end, may well be (mostly) the one given by St Mark, Surbiton, for use in the mission church.

with lighted candles precedes the Vicar as he comes to the steps of the chancel to read the Gospel set for the day. The Creed is sung by all to the setting by John Merbecke. During the paragraph "And was incarnate" everyone kneels, and at the end of the Creed some make the sign of the cross as they declare belief in the life of the world to come. The Vicar climbs the steps of the handsome pulpit, another relic of Southwark, to deliver the sermon. St Olave's is not a church for those who hope for a lengthy exposition of scripture, for the sermon is but a part of the morning's liturgy, and not a centrepiece as it might be in churches of a different persuasion; fifteen minutes at most is a likely duration.

A third hymn is sung while the Vicar prepares the altar for the ritual later in the service. No collection is taken: many of the congregation have already placed in a box at the entrance an envelope that contains their weekly gift for maintenance of the church and for missionary work. Others, who do not take part in this Duplex scheme, have put coins in a separate box. The service moves on through the Prayer for the Church, the Confession and Absolution, and the Comfortable Words. Music begins again with the chanting of "Lift up your hearts" and continues with the *Sanctus* ["Holy, holy, holy"] and *Benedictus* ["Blessed is he"].

After the Prayer of Humble Access, the priest, at the altar with his back to the congregation, starts the prayer that consecrates bread and wine as the Body and Blood of Christ. Bells ring after the words "in remembrance of me". After "Amen", the priest receives a consecrated wafer, and wine from the chalice, while the choir sings the *Agnus Dei* ["O Lamb of God"]. We might expect at this point to see people moving from their seats to receive the Sacrament, but there is little movement, apart from two servers who receive, and from three or four evidently infirm adults who do so too.

The Lord's Prayer is chanted, and "Glory be to God on high" sung to *Merbecke*; the priest blesses the congregation, and then, an Anglo-Catholic addition to the Prayer Book, comes the Last Gospel, or the first fourteen verses of St John's Gospel. The procession of choir and servers leaves the chancel as Mr Sargent, the organist, plays a voluntary. It is a little over an hour since the service began; conversations begin, at least outside the building, before people go home, but there is no provision of refreshments to follow the service.

On another Sunday we are only able to go to church for Evening Prayer, or Evensong. We are surprised to see so many people here at 6.30 p.m., two hundred or so. Today happens to be the festival of a major saint, so that the service will be more elaborate than usual. The choir, servers and clergy enter as we saw before, but the Vicar is wearing a full cloak, or cope. Then the choir and the servers with their lighted candles go before the clergy in a solemn procession around the church, while the first hymn is sung. The Vicar's cope is supported at its corners, train-like, by two boys. This ceremonial aroused disapproval from worshippers in the early years of St Olave's, but has continued on special occasions.

When all have returned to their places, Evensong begins with the chanting of "O Lord, open thou our lips"; the 1928 book has allowed the Vicar to dispense with the introduction prescribed in the 1662 Book of Common Prayer. The Revised Psalter has also permitted a reduction in the number of psalms to be sung; today there are two, well led by the choir, which has now mastered the pointing, or fitting of words to the music of a chant, that its first members found difficult. The congregation sits during the psalms, and is not expected to join in singing, though they stand for the *Gloria* at the end of each psalm.

The first Lesson, or reading, is declaimed from the lectern, and then there is another hymn, before the *Magnificat* is chanted, this time with participation from the congregation, who know the words and the pointing, if not today's chant. Evensong continues as set out in the Prayer Book, with chanted responses and collects [prayers set for the day]. Since today is a Feast Day, the choir sings an anthem, "Lord of all power and might", and for the prayers that follow it the Vicar is able to choose from those newly provided in 1928, as well as from those set in 1662. After a third hymn Mr Davis preaches the sermon; after the final hymn the Vicar blesses the congregation, and the service comes to an end. The lights are now on, a little dim in their metal shades, and the worshippers go out into streets that are nowadays lit, if not brightly, and some perhaps reminisce about the early days of darkness and mud in Long Thornton before they reach their front doors.

We may now return from 1933 and look a little at the evidence for this reconstruction of past events. Most of the above has documentary support. There were changes as the 1930s progressed: incense came to be used, and a plainsong chant replaced the first hymn at the Sung Eucharist. *Merbecke* is assumed as the main service music, only because this setting was thought suitable for the congregation to use, without choir, at the Parish Communion introduced in 1938, which might imply familiarity. Canon Gale provided music for the choir, but we do not know what it was, nor exactly what was said and what was chanted or intoned.

Though some of Fr Haslam's parishioners objected to Anglo-Catholic ceremonial, no one seems to have complained about the form of the Communion rite used and its deviations, mostly derived from the 1928 Prayer Book, from the rite printed in the 1662 Book of Common Prayer. The deletions (the full Ten Commandments and the Exhortations) and additions became part of a liturgical pattern that was used in many churches and cathedrals for decades, inaccurately known as the Prayer Book service, and codified as the Series One alternative service in the late 1960s.

Three additions, used increasingly in Anglo-Catholic churches during the nineteenth century, *Kyrie*, *Benedictus* and *Agnus Dei*, are never mentioned in pre-war documents, either as matters of fact or as items of controversy: *Kyrie* was permitted in the 1928 Book, but only as an alternative to the Summary of the Law which certainly *was* used at St Olave's; *Benedictus* was optional in the 1928 Book; *Agnus Dei*, if used as a "hymn" after the end of the Prayer of Consecration, had been allowed at least since the Lincoln Judgement of 1890,[1] so the probability must be that at least two of these items were sung at the 11 a.m. Eucharist. Whether they were choir-only is also unknown, though later practice at the church suggests that they might have been so.[c] The Preparation and Last Gospel had originally been said inaudibly, but the Church Council voted in 1931 that they should be heard by the congregation.

Churches with the Duplex system were sometimes thought to have no collection, but this was not usually true; amounts of loose collections are recorded in the St Olave's service registers. The length of the main service was once stated as one hour and four minutes—too exact to be a weekly occurrence! This duration probably owed its brevity to the lack of communicants; had all the people received the sacrament, the service would have lasted rather longer. The attendance figure of two hundred in the evening was given in an official return to the Bishop; the morning service attendances can only be estimated,[d] since only the number of communicants, usually in single figures, was recorded.

---

c) By 1961 there was an "extensive repertoire of *Kyrie*, *Sanctus* and *Agnus* settings". (*SON* 12/61)

d) See pp. 68–9.

ILLUSTRATIONS

1. Lane near Lonesome, *c.*1910.

Lambeth Archives Department

2. Mission Church and Hall exterior, 1928.

3. Mission Church and Hall, interior, 1928.

4. Mission Church and Hall, interior, 1928.

5. Fr Haslam, 1930.

6. A. C. Martin, 1930.

7. Laying the foundation stone, 1930.

8. South elevation of the church as planned, 1930.

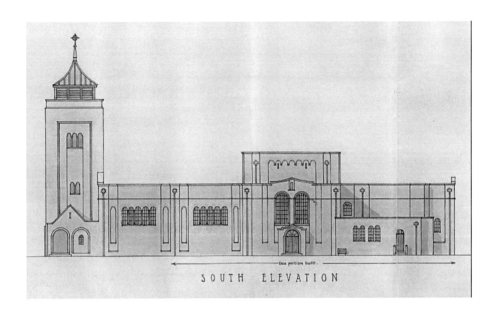

SOUTH ELEVATION

9. South elevation as built, seen in 1960.

10. Interior, *c.*1933.

11. Avenue Road, *c.*1928.

12. Choir with Fr Haslam, 1930.

13. Servers with Fr Haslam, 1930.

Copyright of Surrey History Centre

14. Interior, 1935-40.

15. St Olave, Southwark: from Tooley Street, *c.*1924.

Southwark Local History Library

16. St Olave, Southwark: interior looking W, 1918.

City of London, London Metropolitan Archives

17. Rainwater hopper on the Mitcham church.

Anglo-Catholicism has its origins in the clergy who, from the 1830s onwards, believed that the Church of England was part of the universal Catholic Church, a sacred society rather than a department of the British state. Such clergy argued that the English church had lost a true understanding of Catholic teaching, and one outcome important to St Olave's was the importance given to the service of Holy Communion or Mass. At the same time a movement began to restore to churches furnishings and fittings that used to be there, and to conduct services with ritual and vestments such as had been used in England before the time of the Reformation in the late 1540s. All this provoked much animosity from those who thought that the Church of England was being led back to Popery. This strong anti-Roman nationalism can be seen in the debates about the Prayer Book discussed in Chapter 6.

"High" became the shorthand for Anglo-Catholic, but usually only in connection with the ritual and practices of worship, as was seen in Chapter 7. Since Fr Haslam's time much High practice, if not doctrine, has become the norm, whilst Roman practice has become more Anglican.[a]

To classify levels of Anglo-Catholic practice, Canon John Gunstone devised a system that uses the colours of the spectrum: red, orange, yellow, green, blue indigo, violet:[1] Red is full-faith Papalist: priests want the Church of England reunified with the Church of Rome; they are unmarried; they wear vestments of Roman style; their Sunday Mass may well use parts, at least, of the Roman Catholic Mass, perhaps in Latin; they are called "Father"; both outdoors in the parish and in church they wear the soutane, or continental-style cassock, and the biretta, symbol of the Anglo-Catholic activists within the Church of England. Violet is only just different from the 'plain' Church of England. From Orange to Yellow the Roman influence declines, but there are Prayer Book Catholics who accept many of the doctrines and practices of the Red group, but who in their services mostly follow the Book of Common Prayer and who use ceremonies and vestments of the English or Sarum style publicised from 1899 through Revd Percy Dearmer's *The Parson's Handbook,* which ran to twelve editions.[b]

This classification places St Olave's in the middle area of the Red–Yellow sector, at least until the period just before war began. Fr Haslam had problems in introducing, first, the general tone of Anglo-Catholic

a) See Yates for a succinct account of the history; Yelton and Stephenson for the world of the Red sector and later changes.

b) See Anson, pp. 307–12 for an account of Dearmer's influence.

worship of a moderate kind and, later, some specific items: incense and a statue of Mary. Confession, a cause for objection in 1930, was being "used more" by 1934, but had no regular place in the list of services. Communion was to be received while fasting. A Requiem Mass took place weekly from 1936. His position needs some qualification: he praises the 1928 Book and uses the word "extremist" to describe both Protestant and Anglo-Catholic opponents; he prefers "Mass" as the title for the main Sunday service, but after protests uses the Prayer Book title, "Holy Communion" (though later "Sung Eucharist" is used, too), and conducts the service according to the rite prescribed in the Book of Common Prayer, with additions and subtractions permitted by the 1928 Prayer Book; he uses the 1928 Baptism service and the shortened form of Evensong from that book; he is keen to introduce Reservation, but does not try to add Benediction. It is not possible to say whether this last was on principle or on pragmatic grounds of what would be accepted. In two formal photographs he is wearing a biretta [Red], which he may or may not have worn during services. In the same photographs he wears a Sarum double-breasted cassock [Yellow–Violet], which he may or may not have worn when out and about in the parish.

Shortly before war began, the church adopted more decidedly Anglo-Catholic, non-Prayer Book, names for some of its services: "Ante-Communion" became the "Mass of the Presanctified" and included the Reproaches and the Veneration of the Cross; Easter began with "New Fire" ceremonies on Easter Eve. The Feast of the Assumption appeared in the calendar. The Holy Week and Easter services became more elaborate and the music somewhat more austere and non-congregational—the service on Good Friday, 1940, was sung unaccompanied—and the trend continued after the War, with more plainsong used. Fr Haddelsey walked the parish in soutane, cloak and biretta, and the congregation became, for a time, more of an eclectic one,[2] an Anglo-Catholic centre, but perhaps less of a parish church.

War in 1939 halted, for the time being, the relentless urbanisation of the parish created in 1928 and divided in 1936. Much of that development happened in the earlier years, from 1926 to 1932, moving eastwards towards Pollards Hill. The area retained plenty of open space, much of it occupied by the cemeteries. There were several private sports clubs and grounds, as well as the Tooting Bec [later, Pollards Hill] golf course, though much of this land was sold for housing during the period. The Improvement Association had a playing field and pavilion at the end of Middle Way; the Rowan Road School had its own playing field, and the local authority formed recreation grounds off Grove Road, off Rowan Road and in Sherwood Park.[a] At the edge of the parish boundary the Mizen market gardens continued in production, and Pain's firework factory, inside the boundary, spread across open, tree-lined grounds.

Public buildings included the schools built by Surrey County Council and the East Ward Maternity Centre, or Welfare Clinic, in Meopham Road. Off Rowan Road, the cemetery company opened a crematorium in 1936. Light industry grew, whilst the older, environmentally offensive chemical works at Lonesome declined and closed.

Older cottages, villas and terraces were to be found on the outskirts of the parish, but roads of privately built, brick and red-tiled houses formed into terraces characterised the area. The local authority built an estate of double tenement houses [maisonettes] in 1930–1,[b] and private builders added two small roads of similar housing in 1939, but the boom in flats and maisonettes had yet to come. Shops at the crossing of Northborough Road and Rowan Road completed the picture.

Many new houses were built by Wates, based in Norbury; several local companies were formed and re-formed to build houses, including Joseph Owen's Tamworth Park Construction Company and Fulfords, created to build the Long Thornton Park estate. Permission to build was awarded, and sometimes refused, by Mitcham Urban District Council, acting in accordance with regulations from the Department of Health. Even then, the active involvement of councillors in both the building companies and in the voting of subsidies caused eyebrows to rise.

Without the Council's active promotion of itself as a provider of subsidies and mortgages, very little would have been built. Following a modification in 1923 of the Small Dwellings Acquisition Acts, local councils were empowered to subsidise houses up to £1,200 in value through payments of up to £75 per house, directly to a freehold buyer,

----

a) The recreation ground off Northborough Road, though inside Mitcham, was bought by the Croydon local authority in 1931.

b) The estate was planned in the 1920s, as stated in Montague, but it was first occupied in December 1931. (*UDC* 12/01/32)

or to the builder, for houses to be bought with a mortgage. They could offer a mortgage of up to 90% of the market value of such houses. The Public Works Loan Board lent money to the councils, who added a surcharge to cover the costs of administration when they loaned to buyers. From 1923 the UDC paid subsidies of £75 to builders who would erect houses of less than £600 freehold price, including the subsidy, and provided twenty-year 90% mortgages at (usually) 5¼% interest. By 1931, when the Council decided to discontinue the operation of the Act, £2¼m had been lent to over 4,000 house purchasers.[1]

Builders advertised in the *Evening News* and stressed that purchase was cheaper and better than paying rent. A Fulfords house, of "substantial and pleasing elevation" priced after subsidy at £575 could be had freehold for a deposit of £60, and a Wates house in Sherwood Park for £675.[2] Demand was great: one unnamed builder said "We cannot build them fast enough."

Buses provided transport to Streatham Common station for Southern Railway electric trains to London, but municipal trams in London Road were a longer walk away. The earliest residents experienced three winters of appalling road conditions; developers left roads unmade until the local authority adopted them and provided the proper surfacing. The mud, and the paths made with railway sleepers, drew wide-ranging comparisons: "The avenues and terraces ... are reminiscent of the Giant's Causeway or the shell-holed roads of Flanders during the period of the war." Parents refused to send children to school through "quagmires of mud". The unmade roads and the shortage of school places caused residents to form the Long Thornton Park Ratepayers' Association.[c] Road-surfacing and lighting the streets ran on into 1930, but the *News* thought that, once trees had been planted, Long Thornton would be "one of the most charming residential districts within many miles of London".

Who were the people who inhabited Fr Haslam's parish? Statistics are scarce: though the 1931 Census provides figures for the East Ward of Mitcham, that entity included already established areas of population at Lonesome and Eastfields. The Ward population grew from 6,571 in 1921 to 18,633 in 1931; Fr Haslam expected the Parish population to be 8,500 in June 1929 and recorded it as 14,000 in 1936.[3] Over the full Mitcham UDC area the population grew again by 2.8% from 1931 to 1939.

The population was certainly young: the Charter Day Souvenir of 1934 described an influx to Mitcham mainly of families with young children, and Fr Haslam reckoned that 75% of the children were "infants".[4] The number of children caught Surrey County Council's

---

c) This was the original title; by 1932 it had become the Long Thornton and District Improvement Association Ltd.

Education Committee unawares, and belated new provision included 720 places for older children at Rowan, a school at Sherwood Park, both initially in temporary classrooms, and extra accommodation at Lonesome [two rooms for fifty children each!]. In 1928–9 there were thought to be four hundred children resident in the first estates, whilst in 1929 the Education Committee conceded that there were no places for eighty children; a Ratepayers' Association official claimed that two hundred aged 7½ had still not started school.[5] The adult population, too, was younger rather than older:[d] Councillor Field noted the "earnest and enthusiastic lot of young people" at a Ratepayers' Association meeting in 1927, and the Association's officers seem, to judge from newspaper pictures, to have been men in their forties.

In a sample[e] of 94 male householders in Long Thornton from the 1928 electoral registers, 30 were aged 31–35, with 20 from each of the 21–25 and 35–40 ranges. The same sample gives some idea of where the first residents came from: 65 were born in the London County Council area, 5 in the non-LCC parts of the Metropolitan Police area and 24 outside London.[f] This, of course, does not show where they lived immediately before moving to Long Thornton; records kept by Wates of Streatham suggest that almost all their buyers moved from older properties elsewhere in London.[6] The men in the sample were all born in England, and, with a mortgage dependant on having secure employment, one might expect many residents already to have had jobs in London prior to moving. Of those who had bought homes through Mitcham UDC's mortgage scheme 76% were reckoned in 1927 to have come from outside Mitcham.[7] Thornvale in the *Advertiser* thought at the end of 1928 that Londoners formed a surprisingly small percentage of the population, even suggesting that Northerners predominated. Having met Irish and Scottish residents, Thornvale thought that "a census of nationalities in Long Thornton would provide some interesting statistics." The 2011 census would have interested him even more.

Reasonable assessments can be made of the socio-economic status of the general run of the population, though descriptions provided in documents can be confusing, because of the terminology used by the writers. Fr Haslam and Fr Haddelsey both used "working class" to

---

d) See Table A for comparison between Mitcham UDC and Croydon RDC populations.

e) The sample was made by selecting male householders (their surnames did not change at marriage) who had names unusual enough to be identifiable in the index of births and in the Censuses of 1891 and/or 1901.

f) In corroboration, of the 82 people, male and female, confirmed in 1936–9 at The Ascension, just over half had been baptised, probably as infants, in parishes within the LCC area.[14]

describe the parishioners, and Fr Haslam used "artisan" as a qualifier. The Vicar of The Holy Redeemer classified his parishioners as "artisan and black-coated", which describes what can be shown from limited evidence, that most men were skilled or semi-skilled manual workers or above-basic clerks in commerce or finance.[8]

Fr Haslam's use of "working class" may seem surprisingly undiscriminating in view of his years in Walworth, an area of greater poverty than Long Thornton; nevertheless, the householders of the new estate were weekly wage-earners,[9] rather than monthly paid, salaried employees. This distinction reflected rank within an industry or business, and "salary" had connotations of superior social class. Mitcham UDC, the near-universal mortgage provider, recognised the practical implications of the wages economy by arranging to collect payments in cash at the Meopham Road Clinic, where in one session in 1929 £5,000 was paid in by householders, guarded by a solitary policeman.[10]

The new houseowners[g] of the 1920s had to be at the top end of working-class income to have any chance of repaying the mortgage. With repayments of 18s. to £1 per week over a 15-year period,[h] a married man with children would have struggled on much less than £4 10s per week. Skilled technicians, foremen and clerks of ten or more years of employment with a secure employer would be typical occupations for men in the lower range of mortgagees, with earnings up to £5 10s. per week.[11]

Once mortgage rates fell in the early 1930s and repayment periods extended to twenty-five years, house ownership became more of a possibility for manual workers. Electoral registers show houses with adult occupants with surnames different from those of the husband and wife, perhaps relatives or lodgers, both sources of income once the applicant had satisfied the mortgage provider of the amount and security of his own income. Unhappily, from 1929 economic conditions brought an accelerating number of mortgage defaulters.[12]

A survey of fathers' occupations recorded in the church baptism register confirms the artisan-and-clerk distribution of employment. Of these, 46% could be classified in census terms as "intermediate non-manual workers" and "junior non-manual", 44% as skilled or semi-skilled manual workers. The sample is, of course, small and ignores the childless and those who did not seek baptism for their children;

---

g) Mortgagees were all male, though some houses appear to have been bought outright by women.

h) Fulfords claimed a total of 21s. 2d. per week for "all outgoings"—repayments, rates and insurance—for their houses in Long Thornton Park.[15]

nevertheless, the size of the percentages quoted suggests that the sample is not wholly misleading as a confirmation of the "artisan" label.[i]

Long Thornton was thus a place of first-time buyers, many of whom migrated from suburbs closer to the centre of London, and Fr Haslam's successor in Walworth noted in 1929 that "respectable church families" were moving out into the new districts.[13] It also became a place that some people soon left; removals caused concern within the church even by 1931, since those who left had been committed to the church and had paid their weekly offerings. The departures might imply the purchase of larger, dearer houses elsewhere by people with incomes above the repayment minimum, but there may well be other explanations.

Holidays in mainland Europe became more common, and the two-week group holiday for nearly forty people in Switzerland in 1929 suggests that some within the church congregation had income to spare. The cost was advertised at around £10, and of the tour for 1936 at just over £12.[j] This, though, is no evidence for suggesting that the church congregation was in general or in part more affluent than the average parish resident.

---

i) There is a list of occupations once held by men seeking re-employment in Munday, p. 8.

j) These are group rates: the 1936 trip would have cost around £636 at 2010 prices (MeasuringWorth.com).

58

16: ADDITION AND SUBTRACTION 1935–6

Just as the communicant numbers were approaching what turned out to be their peak, and as final repayment of the debt on the new church came in sight, two projects simultaneously demanded yet more energy and money. The increase in population in the parish led to the creation of a new District, called The Ascension, from within St Olave's parish, whilst the Bishop of Southwark rightly saw that a full-size vicarage had to be provided for St Olave's, either for use as a clergy house for more than one priest, or as a dwelling for a married priest and family. Neither project had the whole-hearted support of both Vicar and Church Council; combined, they damaged the financial stability of St Olave's for several years.

The population of the south-eastern part of the parish was estimated in 1934 to be 4,800, with a further 3,000 dwellings expected.[1] Fr Haslam asked the Bishop for a site for a new church and hall in the Pollards Hill and Sherwood Park areas and for a priest to work in the new District. A site had been found by September 1934, and a building committee, to include parishioners who lived in the area of the new District, was elected. Although the Church Council made it clear that it could not help to finance any new buildings, in January 1935 a Finance Committee heard that the Church Council was to be asked for £500 out of a total of £3,000[a] towards the new District's church and for £50 p.a. towards the stipend of the Priest-in-Charge. This demand, nearly the cost of a house, may well have seemed unfair as well as alarming, because, when St Olave's was founded, its parent church, St Mark's, made no such contribution. St Mark's in 1928, though, had been "under a cloud of financial difficulties", and the days of the Twenty-five Churches Fund had passed; people in the new District, wrote Fr Haslam, could "never hope to receive the generous assistance from outside the parish that we ourselves did."

By the end of 1934 the debt on St Olave's had nearly been repaid. A Gift Day in 1935 almost covered it, and the Church Council resolved in June to pay off what remained. The new demands, though, needed new money. For The Ascension the immediate way of raising money was a two-day Autumn Fayre in 1935, though Fr Haslam personally had hoped to have no more fairs, because of the distraction from visiting and evangelism that they brought. He also had to surrender his "long cherished idea" to have the Lady Chapel built as A. C. Martin had intended.

---

a) £3,000 was reported to St Olave's Church Council, but Fr Sibellas wrote that the Diocese had granted £2,000 as 90% of the cost, which would thus have been about £2,200.[5] For a comparison, the new hall of the Improvement Association, with dance floor and seating for 322 cost £2,650 in 1937.[6]

The Building Committee proposed to concentrate on a hall, as had been done at St Olave's, but Fr Haslam looked for the building of at least a part of a church. By October it was clear that a hall was all that the available grants could support, although Terence Carr also designed a church to be built later.[b] Fr Leonard Sibellas became the Priest-in-Charge from 1 July 1935, and evening services began in the Pollards Hill Central School, until the hall, with seating for up to 200 people,[c] "cheap, convenient and truly devotional",[2] was dedicated by the Bishop on 23 May 1936.

At between two and three thousand pounds the new hall may or may not have been cheap; it was certainly more expensive and more substantially built than the hall/church provided earlier at St Olave's. Exactly what became of the expectation that St Olave's would provide £500 is not clear (the accounts for 1935 and 1936 are not available): the 1935 Fayre raised £157, but there is no mention of a further one, and the 1936 Gift Day income went to the vicarage and to church redecoration. The hall of The Ascension was cleared of debt by its own Gift Day in 1937. There were signs of strain in the parent parish: a last-minute proposal for a Christmas Fair in 1936 was voted down, though gift boxes were provided; a meeting in 1936 agreed that St Olave's should no longer be responsible for hire charges for the Pollards Hill School, and heard that the Church Council was legally obliged to continue its contribution of £50 per year to the new priest's stipend.[d] Even after the hall had been opened, St Olave's remained responsible for the upkeep of The Ascension vicarage. The Council ran into deficit in 1936, and authority was given to raise an overdraft of up to £100, just a year after coming out of debt—though the St Olave's vicarage was blamed for this.

At the same time as the financial demands on St Olave's were increasing, the congregation, and thus the church's income, declined, mainly because of people in the Sherwood Park area who now went to The Ascension. Fr Haslam said that, in view of the division of the parish, St Olave's had done well; the writer of the minutes of the annual meeting of 1937 put it more bluntly, perhaps betraying some resentment: The Ascension had "robbed us of some of our income".

The same Finance Committee meeting that heard of the sums needed for The Ascension also found out that the parish was expected to find

---

b) A sketch was printed in *News* 04/10/35. Not until 1953 was the church of The Ascension consecrated.

c) The anonymous writer in *SDG* noted the "real enthusiasm" of the people and gave 200 as the number of seats. *EC* 93689 gives 100–150.

(d) The Ecclesiastical Commissioners granted £120 p.a. in 1934–5, raised a year later to £150.[7]

£700, in annual instalments, towards the cost of a new vicarage.[e] The Bishop had in December 1934 expressed his wish for a more adequate vicarage; by March 1935 the scheme had been postponed, presumably because of the overwhelming demands for fresh funding. The Church Council did, however, agree that a garage for Fr Haslam's car was essential and for £37 had one built. Although Fr Haslam did not want a vicarage to live in, the Bishop insisted, because of the need to provide for future appointments to the parish.

The eventual cost of the vicarage was £2,300: over half of the funds came from and through the Ecclesiastical Commissioners, but £100 came as a gift from Fr Haslam and his sister, with another £100 from the South London Church Fund. Terence Carr was again the architect and Hudson Brothers of Clapham Junction were the builders. Work eventually began in February 1937, and the house was blessed by the Bishop of Kingston on 24 July. Fr Haslam made it clear that the house really belonged to the parish, and only lived there for a few months. His married successor made it available for meetings of church organisations, and the Commissioners paid £100 for a garden to be laid out according to Mrs Haddelsey's instructions.[3]

By late 1938 the Church Council was responsible for the repairs, decoration and insurance of three houses: the new vicarage, the vicarage of The Ascension District and 44 St Olave's Walk, where Fr Harrison[f] resided. Although the Bishop said in 1934 that there was a chance of selling the present "most inadequate house" to help finance the new vicarage,[4] and Fr Haslam thought the house would become available for letting,[g] neither of these options seems to have been pursued further, and St Olave's offered this house on behalf of the Diocese to a curate until 1967.

---

e) The parish of St Mark, Mitcham, contributed rather less towards the new vicarage built there in 1929–30.[8]

f) Fr Harrison was the first of the curates to be a married man; this may have required the continued use of 44 St Olave's Walk as a clergy house. The first two curates had lodged in local houses, as did the deaconesses.

g) As some compensation the Church Council gained income from renting out the garage.

The first people of St Olave's had to find money for the upkeep of the mission church and then raise large sums for a costly new church; there were no endowments. From 1928 to 1935 all was success, a prodigious achievement in regular giving and in fundraising through special events, but the demands of building a vicarage and a new mission church put the finances into deficit, with an annual instalment of debt to repay.

Church finances after the First World War were in a precarious state: Bishop Garbett's priority was to raise the stipends of clergy in Southwark to an acceptable level,[1] whilst churches in Mitcham were in debt or only just paying their expenses. Mitcham Parish Church, whose Vicar wrote that "we must get rid of the idea that the Church is rich,"[2] was £100 in debt in 1929;[3] St Mark's, Mitcham, was still dealing in 1930 with a debt from 1920.[4] Anglican churches, even if they still had funding through annual subscribers or through rentals for the use of a family pew, had to rely on weekly cash collections and on money-raising events. Collection income could not be predicted, so budgets could not be produced. The parish priest was paid from various sources, usually none of them local, but the congregation was expected to make an Easter Offering as a supplement to his income.

Though the endowments of the Ecclesiastical Commissioners financed clergy stipends, there was no such financial foundation for a new parish's other expenditure.

Regular Giving

The Duplex envelope scheme aimed to address the need for regular giving to churches. The individual or family that signed up to this received a pack of numbered pairs of envelopes: one of the pair was labelled "Maintenance", the other "Extension" [missionary work at home or abroad]. Suggested weekly amounts were displayed on the membership form, but the donor's choice was not in any way guided. "Maintenance" always generated larger sums, but "Extension" at least ensured that the parish looked outside itself, and year by year gave to mission funds, mainly the Society for the Propagation of the Gospel. Fr Haslam hoped that he would be relieved of immediate anxiety about the finances and that normal expenditure would be covered, without the need for fairs or other special fundraising events.

Two hundred sets of envelopes were purchased, ready for a start in December 1929;[h] initially, 136 people signed up, and by early 1931 nearly all sets had been taken, though by the end of that year there were twenty vacancies. The system soon doubled the amounts that had previously been given in unplanned loose collections. Then, as now,

---

h) Mitcham Parish Church introduced Duplex shortly afterwards.

some people were more diligent in their offerings than others; some fell behind and others lapsed altogether. There were several appeals for new members, particularly from the young and newly employed; more difficult was the replacement of established donors who moved away from the area. Whereas in 1929 the scheme was a novelty in a District that was collectively establishing itself, five years later it was common among the committed, and it perhaps needed some effort to persuade others to join in. Unfortunately, when the demands for capital outlay came in 1935–6, the regular giving was also starting to decline.

THE CHURCH DUPLEX FUND.

MEMBERSHIP FORM.

Until I give notice of withdrawal I will contribute regularly each week the amounts marked by crosses in the spaces below.

(The vacant spaces are for amounts other than those shown.)

This side for Maintenance.				This side for Extension.			
WEEKLY OFFERING.				WEEKLY OFFERING.			
£1	10/-	5/-		£1	10/-	5/-	
2/6	2/-	1/-	6d.	2/6	2/-	1/-	6d.
3d.	1d.	½d.	¼d.	3d.	1d.	½d.	¼d.

"Upon the first day of the week (*Systematically*) let every one of you lay by him in store (*Individually*), as God hath prospered him (*Proportionately*), that there be no gatherings when I come." *I Cor. 16, 2.*

"Seek ye first The Kingdom of God, and His Righteousness; and all these things shall be added unto you." *S. Matt., 6, 33.*
"Go ye into all the world and preach the Gospel to every creature." *S. Mark, 16, 15.*

Full Name and Surname..

(Mr., Mrs. or Miss).

Address..

....

Date..

Please tear off this page after filling it up, put it into an envelope and place it in the box in Church, or send it sealed up to your District Duplex Treasurer, Mr. Pascall, 66, Beckway Road, Norbury, S.W.16.

Those who did not participate in Duplex could, of course, contribute in cash as and when they came to church; after a peak of £111 in 1931, the first year of the new church, and good years in 1933–4, such income settled to about £60 p.a. in the later 1930s. Donations at occasional services suggest that the 'loose change' mentality was still strong among infrequent worshippers and those not committed to Duplex: the Harvest Festival in 1933, held on a weekday evening, attracted four hundred or so people, but the collection totalled £6 0s. 6d., or about 3½d. per person.

Proportionate giving, as is now promoted in the Diocese of Southwark, had not developed in the Church of England eighty years ago; the model of regular, committed giving was in itself new, and it would take a lot to change the perception that church finance was a matter of special appeals, Easter Offerings, fairs and sales of work, and loose change in the Sunday collection. Nevertheless, it may be worth asking how much, proportionately, people gave, in humble recognition that the first residents were not very prosperous and lived in a decade that began with unemployment and lowered incomes. On the basis of the peak income of the Duplex scheme of £460 in 1934 and, say, 170 fairly regular envelope users, we arrive at an average of £2 14s. 0d. per set per year, or around one shilling a week. If that shilling were the result of applying today's recommendation of giving at a rate of 5% of income, it would derive from a gross income of one pound a week, whereas many householders in the social groups represented in Long Thornton earned five pounds or more per week and had to pay around eighteen shillings to one pound a week for the mortgage.[5] Table C suggests that regular givers today, though smaller in number, may give more. On the other hand, cash collection income now is about a quarter of what was given in the 1930s.

Proportionality aside, the shilling average was enough for the parish's needs,[i] and Duplex provided financial security through its reminder to give <u>regularly</u>, however much the individual amounts. Those who used it were almost certainly giving in other ways, to the building fund, the organ fund, gift days and collections for sundry worthy causes, besides giving their time and talents to the large-scale fundraising events; in 1930, for example, goods to the value of £140 were donated to the new church. The Duplex income did indeed cover all the costs of wages, salaries and maintenance; what it never did was develop into a fund for the future. In 1932 it was agreed to set aside an annual sum for repairs, but that never happened regularly, if at all.

The practice of making an Easter Offering to the Vicar continued at St Olave's. Amounts varied from £13 to £16, and Fr Haslam always gave his Offering income back to church funds.

The hall, far from being a source of income, remained stubbornly in deficit, despite many discussions about hire charges and economy measures. It seems to have been used solely by church or connected youth groups, who were charged preferential rates that did not even cover the cost of heating and lighting. Wider hiring was discouraged by a concern that the UDC would then levy rates on the hall. Moreover, in 1934 the Church Council resolved that no parties, dances or whist drives were to be held there during Lent.

---

i) Fr Sibellas suggested this rate to reluctant contributors at The Ascension.[9] One shilling could pay for a couple to have an evening out at the cinema.

Fundraising

The Church Building Fund began straight away in 1928 and accumulated £332 in that year alone, with another £394 in 1929. Much of it came from collecting-boxes kept at home; a picture in the magazine each month showed a wall rising, as bricks at sixpence each were subscribed.[j] Sales and fairs, with their attendant concert parties, brought in large sums for the building and for the organ fund: a three-day Fayre in 1929 raised £210, a sum surpassed by fairs in 1930 and 1931. That of 1932 raised £256, but £50 came from straight donations, which encouraged a change of policy away from fairs, thought to be becoming stale, to annual gift days, for which collecting-boxes were issued.[k] Fr Haslam was wary of fairs, because they distracted him from visiting and other evangelistic work (one suspects that the Vicar was expected by some to play a prominent part in arranging such events): "There is nothing wrong about such sales, but they are dangerous when they become ... the main occupation of Christian workers." Thornvale

had doubts: fairs had a social value, and a Norbury church had seen its income drop alarmingly once it dropped its three-day bazaar. Financially, at least, he was right: even in the good year of 1934 the gift day raised £200, less than any fair. Even so, by retail price comparison, the lowest-level indicator, this means £11,100 at 2010 prices;[6] it is hard to imagine how either a fair or a gift day in Mitcham could nowadays raise such a sum. After some years of gift days a two-day fair was planned for 1938; perhaps because such a grand event was by then a novelty, it raised £227, including a donation from Queen Mary.

---

j) See back cover.

k) The Improvement Association's sports ground was partly financed by private loans from residents,[10] and regular whist drives provided income.

Expenditure

Because the church was new, it did not need frequent repairs, though the hall often required attention. Ordinary premises maintenance was mainly done through the church's unemployment fund;[l] no doubt small items were attended to by the Verger.[m] Heating and lighting ran at an annual average of £40 for the church and £30 for the hall, and the Diocese levied a charge of £20–25 per year. Giving to missions peaked at £54 in 1934.

Staffing costs rose to £268 by 1938, because of the employment of curates partly financed by the parish and because their stipends increased during the period. Curates, (including one for The Ascension) each cost the parish £50 towards a stipend of £200, until the appointment of Fr Harrison, who received £255, of which the parish contributed £95, besides paying insurance and property taxes on his house. Because of missing evidence, it is not clear when the parish ceased to pay towards the Priest-in-Charge at The Ascension, or how much the two deaconesses cost the parish, though the drop of staffing costs by £48 in 1939, after Deaconess Trotter had left, might supply a clue. The demands on the parish for Quota [payments made to the central funds of the Diocese] and staffing costs were notably less in pre-war days than they are now.[n]

Two laymen were paid: Geoffrey Sargent, Organist, received £60 per year, and William Carey, Verger, about £47 per year, though his income was always defined in weekly terms, a distinction in status common in the period.

Capital Expenditure and Debt Repayment

Throughout the 1930s the Church Council was repaying debts. Although A. C. Martin's design for the church had been scaled down to match the money potentially available, by 1931 a debt of £1,500 had to be repaid; the Bishop gave five years as a limit, but the parish cleared

---

l) See Chapter 21.

m) His duties included stoking the furnace for heating, keeping the premises tidy, and simply being present to keep a watchful eye on the grounds. He had a ceremonial role, for a gown was provided. It was assumed that such a person was needed; nowadays only more prosperous parishes can afford employees for day-to-day tasks. Indeed, churchwardens now do jobs that Dr Pailthorpe would not have contemplated.

n) See Table D for some details of expenditure on staffing, Quota and missionary work.

the debt in four.[o] It responded again to the challenges of 1935–6, as explained in the previous chapter, but the debt then incurred lingered into the war years, by which time the partition of the parish had left fewer parishioners to share in the repayments. The parish officials of the period did all that they could to be prudent and to encourage responsible giving by worshippers, but they were, one feels, worn down by demands beyond their control.

As a general note, at the end of three chapters concerning money matters, the reader should remember that the usual view of the 1930s as an era of poverty and mass unemployment is inaccurate for London and the Home Counties. There was indeed a difficult patch in 1931–3, even though prices fell at that time; as Fr Haslam observed, "None of us is in a position to give much." However, net incomes increased during the decade, even if wages remained static or with little increase: nationally, money earnings increased by 5.7 points in 1928–38, whereas real earnings increased by 12 points.[7] Some residents owned cars. Mortgage rates for existing holders, on transfer from Mitcham UDC to a building society in 1936, fell from 5¼% to 4½%.[8]

---

o) The amount of interest paid in 1932 was £64. By then the base bank rate had fallen to 2% from a high of 6% in early 1931.[11]

18: SIGNS OF GROWTH

Attendances

Attendance numbers are hard to come by in the 1928–39 period, because the service registers only recorded communicants, whose numbers at the main Sunday service were almost always in single figures, because of the practice of fasting communion, described and discussed elsewhere. In 1932–6 around eighty worshippers a week came to the early morning services of Holy Communion, and we could assume that at least half of these returned for the Sung Eucharist in the late morning, to be joined by people who attended the main service of the day at the usual Anglican hour, but who were not communicants, because of the fasting rule, or because they had never been confirmed; such worshippers were the cause of concern that led to the introduction of the Parish Communion in late 1938.

Evening service numbers reported to the Bishop in 1928 were 150 (but dependant on the state of the unmade roads!) and 200 in 1935.[1] To modern eyes these seem astoundingly high. Even if attendance at Evening Prayer represents a liking for a non-eucharistic service, it seems unlikely that the evening service attracted more people than the morning one at the customary time. We know that the mission church was at least sometimes crowded and had seating for 250 or more;[a] communicant numbers rose once the new church was open, so we could guess at 11 a.m. attendances of 300 or more on normal Sundays. Just under 200 sets of envelopes for the Duplex scheme were issued, to individuals and to families.

Festivals of Christmas and Easter show communicant numbers of around 300–350 in 1935–6, nearly all, of course, at the early morning services or, at Christmas, also at the midnight service, to which the rule of fasting was meant to apply. Christmas Midnight Mass began in 1932 with 128 communicants and peaked in 1934 with 212. Communicant numbers at Easter 1934 included: 25 at 6.15 a.m., 103 at 7.00 a.m. and 176 at 8.00 a.m. The extra communicants were probably regular non-communicating worshippers who received the sacrament at great festivals and made the effort to attend at an early hour, but we do not know how many returned at 11 a.m. We can suppose that, as now, attendances at Christmas and Easter were higher all round, and that therefore the total number of worshippers at the main service of the day rose, so 400 or more would not be impossible. For the Harvest Festival Evensong in 1933 extra chairs had to be brought in from the hall, but by then space had been cleared for an altar in the South transept. The

---

a) See note (b) in Chapter 3.

provision in 1931 of 515 places turned out to be over-generous, at least for normal purposes.

Festival attendances rose at about the same rate as did the parish population and fell accordingly once The Ascension had its priest and building. Regular normal-Sunday communicant numbers never rose at the same rate and, after the division of the parish, fell back to what they had been at the start of housing development in the Sherwood Park area. On the last Easter Sunday before the hall at The Ascension was dedicated, in 1936, the number of communicants roughly matched the number of adults on the electoral roll [350], but the normal Sunday number that year never rose above one-third of the Easter one. Included in the communicants were those confirmed but not yet of an age [eighteen] to be on the roll, so the number of communicant adults was lower than it might seem.

Fr Haslam recorded his pleasure at the growth in communicant life up to the start of 1936,[2] but it is then that a plateau is reached, reflected in further concern about removals from the parish and the loss of valuable church workers. Fr Haslam estimated in 1935 that there were around 500 lapsed communicants in the parish, but these may be either lapsed attenders or attenders who no longer received the sacrament. Again, though, we have no record of attendance numbers beyond communicants. Communicant numbers at the Parish Communion, introduced in late 1938, ranged from 15 to 30, though some of these may have already been communicants who simply changed their time of attendance.

We can use some other indicators of attendance: the electoral roll was 350 in 1936 and 290 in 1938 (after the division of the parish); the parish magazine, sold to non-churchgoers as well, and probably sold per household, rather than to individuals, had a circulation of 700 per month in 1931, but 500 in 1936.[b] The Sunday School roll was 200 in 1928, 400 in 1931 and 500 (300 girls, 200 boys) in 1935.[3] These latter figures surely show that the church had some effect on the local population, and had the volunteers [25 teachers] to manage such large numbers. The children were accommodated, at a cost in hire charges, in the schools at Sherwood Park (from 1929) and Rowan Road (from 1933). Nevertheless, numbers fell to 230 after the division of the parish.

Once The Ascension offered church attendance to those living in the Sherwood Park area, communicant numbers at St Olave's returned to the level that existed in 1931. Although St Olave's had formed and nurtured Christians from that area, who had, for their part, accepted the inconvenient distance which they had to walk, the support for a new District left the parent church deprived of several active members, and

---

b) In comparison, 600 people (from a membership of over 2,500) attended a meeting of the Improvement Association in 1930; its Pavilion Social Club had 500 members in 1937.

those who stayed must surely have noticed the empty spaces. Indeed, in March 1937, after a complaint that the chairs were too close together for comfort, some rows were removed.

Baptism

Whereas the increase in numbers of worshippers and communicants brought unqualified satisfaction, the baptism of a great number of babies caused some misgivings. Fr Haslam used the 1928 alternative order of service which retained the term "Publick Baptism" in its title, whilst the 1662 Prayer Book gave clear instructions that infants were to be baptised during Morning or Evening Prayer on a Sunday, partly so that the adults in the congregation could be reminded of the promises made on their behalf at their own baptisms. Godparents were expected to be practising communicants in the Church of England. By 1928 the custom, the "done thing", as Fr Haslam described it, was that children were brought for baptism (or perhaps the word was "christening") on a Sunday afternoon, and the parents might have no intention of taking any further part in church life. In articles in 1934 and 1936 Fr Haslam reminded godparents of their duties and said that children thus carelessly baptised had "grown up without any understanding of their heritage, their duty, or their responsibility." His views evidently did not pass unchallenged: he admitted in 1936 that "he had been severely criticised," but nevertheless intended to pursue "the standard he thought the church should have".

He was hardly alone in the Church of England in having misgivings: the then Canon Garbett had written a pamphlet for the National Mission of 1916 in which he denounced the "practically indiscriminate administration of the Sacrament" and the "scandal of the existence of thousands of baptised men and women who are utterly ignorant of the bare elements of Christianity".[4] Senior clergy produced an inconclusive report on the subject in 1920, whilst twenty years later an article was published called simply "Baptismal Disgrace". The national statistics were clear: 11½ million babies were baptised in the 24 years up to 1939, but the Easter communicants in 1937 totalled 2¼ million.[5]

The system of baptising the children of anyone in the parish who asked made no demands of preparation or public promise on the parents and godparents, so that the service was not, as it was meant to be, one of initiation into the body of the worshipping church, when the priest declared after the baptism "We receive this child into the congregation of Christ's flock." When in 1930 Fr Haslam did baptise some children during Evensong, as the Prayer Book directed, the *News* called it an "uncommon ceremony". By 1936 the Bishop of Southwark had requested parishes to be "much more particular" in administering baptism.

Contrary to the national trend, baptism numbers rose during the period: 59 in 1928, 83 in 1934 and 98 (St Olave's and The Ascension combined) in 1939. Fr Haslam's house-visiting must have reminded parents of the presence of the Church of England, whilst a leap in numbers in 1931 might suggest more awareness of the church among residents once the new building was visible. However, the local demographic profile of first-time housebuyers who were younger rather than older probably best explains the rise in infant baptisms, and the turnover of residents ensured an inward migration by couples of child-rearing age. Twenty-four adults were baptised, whilst "R.I.P." appears against the names of eight infants, a reminder of the sad duties of a parish priest and of the hazards of birth.

Confirmation

Confirmation, according to the Book of Common Prayer, is the "laying on of hands upon those that are baptised and come to years of discretion". The practice drew criticism from outside the Church of England because "discretion" hardly meant adulthood in the majority of cases, for confirmation in the 1930s was primarily a rite for the under-sixteens, and most candidates were aged eleven to fourteen; Fr Haslam thought eleven to be a suitable age. At St Olave's the clear correlation between names of boys in the confirmation register and those mentioned in the magazines in connection with the choir suggests that confirmation was expected of boys in the choir. Membership of the Boy Scout troop was conditional, at least by 1938, on attendance at Sunday School or Bible Class, so a certain amount of institutional pressure was at work, at least among boys. This directing of "discretion" was not unusual in the period, and only the Holy Spirit can know what were its fruits.

Some over-sixteens, at least in the earlier years, were confirmed, a good sign of adults being brought to faith; not all the new residents brought previous communicant membership with them. However, this small number poses a question: how many adults were in fact confirmed members of the church? As noted earlier, the 300 or so Easter communicants in 1933–4 were outnumbered by the Harvest Festival congregation—though, of course, we have no way of knowing how many of either group were children, or whether children were even counted.

Adrian Hastings quotes from an article of 1928: "The children of well-to-do churchmen are confirmed almost as a matter of course, whereas among the wage-earners confirmation is exceptional."[6] Given the clerk/artisan composition of the parish, it might well be that, even in a would-be Anglo-Catholic church, by no means all the adults were confirmed. We might infer that for some adults the package of confirmation and early-morning communion was not what they wanted, though they could participate in an older (and less Catholic?) routine of

Evensong and Harvest Festival, perhaps along with attendance at the non-communicating Sung Eucharist, since Mattins was not available as the main service of Sunday. Perversely, at that service confirmed and not confirmed were united, because almost none received the sacrament.

Between 10% and 20% per year of those confirmed in 1932–36 lived in the Sherwood Park and Commonside East areas that later fell within the new District of The Ascension; after 1936 those confirmed from St Olave's all lived within the contracted [equivalent to the present-day] parish, except for a small number of those from parishes nearby. Confirmation numbers grew with the population and reached a peak of 83 in 1934. The total of candidates in 1939 from St Olave's and from The Ascension District combined was 57, a decline in line with diocesan and national trends.[c]

Study and Evangelism

Study Circles took place at various times, and perhaps not all were reported. Seventy-five people attended in 1934. Special services in Lent were encouraged. In several years from 1932 retreats were conducted, first for men alone, then for men and women separately.

An open-air service in the Sherwood Park recreation ground was tried in June 1934, but met with a "feeble response" from residents. Though "worthwhile", services in response to the Archbishop's Recall proved similarly disappointing, especially among the younger generation. On the evenings of Good Friday in 1934 and 1935 a procession of witness, organised by Mr Sargent, walked around the parish; Fr Haslam acknowledged that some of those taking part had initially felt uncertain and self-conscious, but thought it a "truly wonderful" occasion.

Fr Haslam's parish work was based on "systematic visiting" of parishioners,[7] which had remarkable results in the first years of the parish, but which he found overwhelming as the numbers increased rapidly and as the turnover of residents began. In 1933 laymen from the church carried out a programme of visiting the newest houses in the parish, and in 1936 all houses were visited to invite non-churchgoers to special services in Lent.

Fr Haddelsey had barely arrived when he called a special meeting to discuss evangelisation: people were to adopt roads and be responsible for the newly confirmed; after a parish-wide letter, there would be mission services in Advent 1938; the daily eucharist should be better supported, and the church used more for prayer. Although the usual signs of the new broom can be detected, it is hard not to feel that the

---

c) See Table B.

energies expended in the period up to the end of 1935, followed by further financial strains and the splitting of the parish, had led to a little weariness. The Church Council, perhaps missing Fr Haslam's chairmanship, spent a lot of time in 1938–9 on details of the 1938 Fayre, the new Vicar's induction service and on the rates to be charged for use of the hall, and felt challenged by damage and vandalism.[d] The Fayre was an occasion for fundraising and raising the profile of the church in the neighbourhood, but it was also a celebration of the recent past,[e] "the phenomenal progress made in the parish of St. Olave, both in the spiritual life of the parish and on the material side in the raising of funds."[8]

---

d) See Chapter 22.

e) See also Chapter 20 for nostalgic comments from 1938.

19: ORGANISTS AND CHOIR

As soon as Fr Haslam began visiting the new homes of Long Thornton, he began recruiting a choir of boys and men[a] to sing in the mission church. Of the boys assembled by Fr Haslam, only one or two had had previous choir experience, and only repetition and rote learning enabled the choir to sing for the dedication of the mission church in January 1928. After the great effort put into this occasion, standards barely improved. Very soon notices in the magazine advertised for boys "with good voices" and implied selectiveness through terms such as "a limited number". A year later the boys' choir numbered twenty-three, described as "unwieldy, not to say unruly", and plans were announced to reduce it to a standing number of eighteen. The men of the choir seem to have been either learners, or more experienced and bored by the inevitable repetitions during choir practices. However, even those with a church background found they had something to learn in the unfamiliar words and tunes of *The English Hymnal*.[b]

There was no money at first to buy musical expertise, so the choir had to be run by local volunteers. Frederick Wood became choirmaster; he was a schoolmaster, which may have helped him to manage the unpromising individuals assembled by Fr Haslam. The organist was Wilfred Honhold, who also led the *Merrie Mountebanks* concert party troupe of entertainers. Mr Wood resigned at the end of 1928 following his appointment both as a Lay Reader and as Headmaster of Christ Church School, Streatham, and Mr Honhold agreed to combine the two musical posts. Although he had given "every assurance of his competence" as an organist, he was perhaps not similarly skilled as a choir trainer (or tamer!), and admitted two months later that progress was slow; attendance at practices by both boys and men was not sufficiently regular, and some of the boys, though provided with a club for recreation, were taking choir practices as "the opportunity for a good rag".

---

a) See Illustration 12 for a picture of the choir in 1930; see Appendix F for a note on church choirs of the period and their educational value.

b) *The English Hymnal*, first published in 1906, became the hymnbook of many Anglo-Catholic churches. Elsewhere in the Church of England, one of the versions of *Hymns Ancient and Modern* was likely to be in use. In a sample of 32 hymns used in the early 1930s, 19 appeared in both books; 5 were found only in *EH*; 5 had words not found in *A&M*; 3 had tunes not in *A&M*. There was a lot to be learnt, and the green hymnbook was another sign that worship at St Olave's was different from that previously experienced by many members of the first congregations.

How matters developed in the next eighteen months is unknown. At the annual meeting in 1930 Mr Honhold was congratulated on his "great success" but by November he had resigned both the voluntary posts that he held. In the meantime he had given up his activity with *The Merrie Mountebanks* on account of his work with the choir and organ. Fr Haslam wrote to him to explain why he could not be appointed permanent paid organist, and the Church Council recorded its "heartiest thanks" for what he had done. A temporary organist was to be employed at a fee of £30 per annum, but the permanent post would be worth £40 per annum, the occupant to be selected by the Vicar.

Mr Honhold's competence may or may not have been an issue. At a presentation ceremony Fr Haslam thanked Mr Honhold for the "wonderful services he did in the old days", which suggests that he thought a change was necessary for the new building and for the future. When challenged by the *News*, he clarified his change of opinion: "As time went on I saw that he did not suit my requirements. The organist must be my right-hand man, and for that position I must have a regular communicant."

Mr Honhold made known his belief that he had been invited to resign because, as he put it, he was not a sufficiently good churchman to have care of the souls of the choirboys. One of his supporters claimed that Fr Haslam would not have the finest organist in the world if he were not "a true Catholic". Mr Honhold's grievance was compounded by some mismanagement or tactlessness by the Vicar and, presumably, the Churchwardens. He assumed that he held a substantive post and declined to compete, whereupon an organist was appointed without any competition, one moreover whose name was meant to be kept secret, though all but stated by a newspaper reporter.

Mr Honhold's supporters were of the party that opposed the Anglo-Catholic trend of worship at St Olave's, so the local press could air two disagreements at once; some of his allies left the church,[c] and then mounted a challenge at the annual meeting in April 1931. They were outnumbered. The Vicar stated his right to appoint an organist and claimed that the change was made "in the highest interests of the church". The applause that greeted his response to the challengers was repeated "thunderously" at the end of the meeting to acclaim the passing of a vote of confidence. We may assume that the majority present had lost any appetite for an old dispute and, probably, that the new appointee was already showing his skill.

The *News* did not reveal the name of Geoffrey Sargent in December 1930, but his identity would have been obvious from the biographical details supplied then and again in January. Aged 29, for seven years he

---

c) Mr Honhold retained some connection with the church; he became the organiser of the Swiss holiday planned in 1931.

had been organist at St Philip, Norbury, after posts elsewhere in the area. He had succumbed to ill health, which made the work there too much for him, and resigned to have a long rest. Dr Pailthorpe, who lived in Norbury, knew him, and he was also a friend of Fr Haslam. Described as "skilful and popular", he was also an Anglo-Catholic in religion, and began his duties at St Olave's with the consecration on 17 January 1931. By April he had started organ recitals; in May the magazine praised his "great ability and untiring energy" and noted that the choir had made "wonderful progress during the last few months". After six months the Church Council agreed to pay the organist £60 per annum, instead of £40, and in early 1932 discussed, inconclusively, organ voluntaries; perhaps some listeners were feeling overwhelmed by unprecedented quality and quantity.

By Christmas 1933 the boys' choir was good enough to sing at St Ann, Gresham Street, in the City: carols, and a service for the Company of Cordwainers. Mr Sargent taught the faith and by 1938 he had formed a Boys' Guild for Scripture; the annual meeting heard of the "keen spirit" in the choir. In 1940 he was commissioned in the Army Survey Department and left St Olave's for the duration of the war. Besides the "exceptionally high musical standard of our truly voluntary choir", Dr Pailthorpe praised him for the "many youngsters whose Christian characters will live as a memorial of his work".

Mr Sargent, by then a Major in rank, returned in 1948 after war service, became MBE in 1951 and remained until 1961, by which time the organ was in poor condition, and the numbers of the choir had diminished.[1] However, one of his last duties was to play the rebuilt instrument at a service of rededication on 25 March 1961. Fifty years later his skilful and delicate accompaniment of plainsong was still remembered.[2] He died in 1972 and a plaque by the organ console records his long service to St Olave's.

20: SOCIAL LIFE

Any suburban Anglican church in the 1930s was likely to maintain several clubs and societies to cater for the interests of different age ranges. Some might be closely defined as religious societies; more would be of general interest. Some would be single-sex, others for male and female. All these organisations needed volunteers to run them, especially those that offered activity for younger age groups; at St Olave's the effort to engage young people before and during adolescence was remarkable. The large fairs and bazaars of that era were social events too, though they needed hard work in preparation. From a later viewpoint the quantity of organized activity is astonishing; we need to remember that free home entertainment through broadcasting had only lately begun and that the cinema in Mitcham, opened in 1933, was not easy of access from Long Thornton. The 1930s were years when outdoor pursuits were popular—rambling and camping, in particular—so we should not be surprised to see these activities in the list of church organizations that were operating in 1938:[1]

Choir and servers: From 1928. Boys and men.

St Olave's Men's Club: Formed 1931. Tuesday evenings at 8 p.m. Indoor recreation for the men of the parish: billiards, snooker, table-tennis, darts, cards, shove-ha'penny, chess and draughts.

Church of England Men's Society: Branch formed June 1936. Once a month. Fellowship for churchmen to spread the influence of the Church.

Women's Fellowship: Formed February 1928. Wednesday afternoons. Speakers invited; open afternoons; an occasional service in Church.

Mothers' Union: Branch formed 1929. Membership: 73. Last Thursday of every month.

St Olave's Guild: Formed 1931. Thursday evenings. For sociability among the youth of the parish, male or female: badminton, table-tennis, dancing. In summer, countryside rambles.

St Olave's Junior Men's Club: for young men aged 14 to 19. Friday evenings. Indoor games, as Men's Club.

King's Messengers: Branch formed 1936. Tuesday evenings. Boys and girls until age 21. Missionary group for young people.

St Olave's Boy Scouts: Formed 1931. Wednesday evenings. Two camps annually. For boys aged 11 to 17, subject to membership of either the Sunday School or Bible Class.

St Olave's Wolf Cubs: For boys aged 8 to 11. Thursday and Friday evenings.

Girl Guides and Rangers: Guide Company formed June 1929; Rangers 1933. Monday evenings.

St Olave's Brownies: Wednesday evenings.

The church choir preceded the Boy Scouts as an organisation for boys. Membership of these two bodies could be combined, and church membership was a requirement for Scouts. However, the Vicar clearly primarily encouraged the choir and played a leading role in the summer camps; in at least one year a camp was run specifically for boys not in the Scouts. There is no evidence of friction or competition for boys' attention between the two groups, as could easily have been the case with no clear church input into the Scouts. Organists in churches could find the Scouts obstructive: in 1930 one wrote that the Scout movement was "not a religious organization" and preferred the Church Lads' Brigade or the Boys' Brigade as movements where there was less likely to be a conflict of loyalties.[2] Such a preference was common among Anglo-Catholic parish priests;[3] The Ascension church had a troop of the CLB.

Besides these established bodies, other clubs and activities came and went. A tennis club met when courts were available: originally on the site where the new church was later built, in 1930 the courts moved next door, at the instigation of Mr Field, on to land later used for the recreation ground. By the end of the next year the club had been wound up. In 1935 Fr Haslam suggested the re-establishment of courts on church land, but the Church Council declined the proposal on grounds of cost.

The "Merrie Mountebanks" concert party was "permanently established" by April 1930, and a "distinctive costume" was being prepared. Their concert in aid of the 1930 Summer Fayre drew praise from the *News* for its "extensive and up-to-date repertoire"; many of the items were "distinctly clever and entertaining". The group faded out, but lived on in memory; a concert in 1938 "took one back to the days when our own 'Mountebanks' kept their audiences convulsed with laughter."

A dramatic society was "in full swing" in 1932, but seems not to have attracted the attention of the local press. The hall was provided with new stage lighting in 1937.

Socials, parties and outings took place several times a year: in the early years we find a Christmas party for 130 children held in the

Meopham Road Welfare Centre; an outing for the choir and servers to a Maskelyne and Devant's performance in London; a Vicar's Social after the consecration of the new church; a Sunday School outing to Box Hill; a social for 320 people in the church hall. Several group visits to Switzerland were organised.

The church, then, was a centre for social activities in the years before the war. However, the Ratepayers'/Improvement Association offered attractions in Middle Way on a larger scale and with better facilities, especially when its new Eltandia Hall was opened in 1937. The Association arranged large-scale events on Bank Holidays, as well as dances on its licensed premises and sports on its field. It did include young people, but never offered the regular meetings of organizations, uniformed and otherwise, that were based at the church. These, and the consequent involvement of siblings and parents, distinguished the church from the Association, which declined in the last years of the 1930s. Its historian suggested that the "very active" church might have drawn some attention of the residents away from the Association.[4]

21: WORTHY CAUSES AND THE WIDER WORLD

Councillor Field noted in early 1933 that unemployment had become "considerable" and that local building schemes had slowed down. The Church Council set up an unemployment fund and invited the congregation to support it; within a month the weekly income was 25s., but the support was not what had been hoped for. To begin with, the fund simply made donations to the Mitcham unemployment fund, but it was then decided that a more direct way of helping would be to employ, at the maximum permitted rate of £1 per week, a man registered as unemployed, who could undertake maintenance works in and around the church and hall. Enthusiasm for this fund declined, and fresh appeals in 1936 met with a "feeble response", even at the asking rate of one penny per week. By then unemployment had fallen,[1] but the fund continued and in 1937 financed the painting of the exterior of the hall; indeed, it was proposed that the name should be changed to "maintenance fund". The church's response to the high unemployment of the early 1930s was small-scale (perhaps there was some donor fatigue), but it was practical and it continued into 1939, having done "a very useful job". The Improvement Association, with a larger membership, ran a more elaborate project and in 1933 distributed relief in kind to the value of £82, rather more than was raised by church members.[2]

Fr Haslam encouraged interest in the League of Nations Union, and the Church Council agreed by a small margin in November 1933 to affiliate to the Union, which promoted the League's aims of disarmament and collective security. Though support for the Union had faltered, it was about to conduct a Peace Ballot in which eleven million people recorded their support for the League.[a] More controversial politics came on the agenda in February 1939, when it was resolved not to hire the hall for use by "a certain political body"; the identity of the body can only be guessed, though Oswald Mosley had spoken at the Baths Hall in Mitcham a year earlier.

The Women's Fellowship in 1933 heard talks on birth control, a subject of debate at the Lambeth Conference of 1930, and, on Fr Haslam's advice,[b] the Church Council declined to comment on the Sunday opening of the cinema in Mitcham. The *News* reported in 1936 a "very large gathering" on 28 January at a memorial service for King George V. Special causes were supported: donations were made in 1934 to the Gresford Colliery Disaster Fund and in 1938 to a fund for

---

a) For more about the Union and the Peace Ballot, see Chapter 6 of Richard Overy, *The Morbid Age* (London 2010).

b) See p. 16.

Jewish refugees from Germany; in 1939 an appeal was to be made following a letter from the Vicar of Tylorstown, a Rhondda mining village.

Although some crisis leaflets were published by the authorities in 1938, there is curiously little reference to the worsening international situation in the church magazine or in the Church Council's minutes. Perhaps this was all part of keeping calm; as Thornvale remarked, "If one were seeking signs of panic, one would have to look elsewhere than in Long Thornton." No doubt churchgoers did as others did, and attended meetings about air raid precautions and gas masks.

22: A FINE TRADITION

Peacetime ended for churchgoers when air raid sirens sounded during the 11 a.m. service on 3 September 1939, at which point this history ends. To write about events from a distance of over seventy years, when St Olave's survives, but with challengingly small attendances, requires some humility. Sadly, few of the Twenty-five churches have latterly flourished as they did in their first years; when reviewing Kenneth Richardson's book, Fr Geoffrey Kirk noted that, of these churches, most built to hold over four hundred worshippers, twenty had congregational counts of eighty or less.[1]

People knew that St Olave's was <u>there</u>: with visiting by clergy and deaconesses and teams of lay people, with processions of witness, Sunday Schools, activities and societies for all ages, well publicised fundraising events, this was not an idle, introspective religious society. A visitor in 1933 noted the "real keenness for the church ... The people love it and look upon it as a spiritual home."[2] Its energy was replicated in the beginnings of The Ascension. Anyone could see the large numbers going to and from the church on Sundays.

Compared simply with the Improvement Association, as a club to join, the church never attracted quite the same numbers. The churches, of course, made demands on their adherents, although they too had their mainly social organisations. The Association, which began from a soapbox speech on the site of the future church,[3] provided social facilities and argued the needs of residents to the UDC. It was a complex organisation run by volunteers, but the years up to 1935 were "the real heyday of the Association",[4] a comment which finds a parallel in the development of St Olave's church, though through The Ascension the Church of England and Anglo-Catholicism continued to expand.

There is no reason to dispute the self-assessment of "phenomenal progress" in the 1938 Fayre programme. A remarkable church building drew hundreds of people to Anglican worship, the congregation created initially through the evangelising energy of the mission priest and loyal helpers. Yet there was an acknowledgement that things were not as they had been. The new Vicar, "always active and restless",[5] clearly found aspects of parish life that needed revival, and hinted at disagreements that needed mending: "It is quite obvious that you are all tremendously keen on your church and its work, but I am sure you will be the first to agree that, like the priest, members of a congregation make mistakes from time to time, with the result that the work of God's kingdom on earth is hindered. These mistakes are usually those which tend to impair the unity of the congregation." There is a fractious tone in some of the minutes of 1939: the Council declined to plant shrubs in the church grounds, because "they would certainly be either stolen or damaged, owing to the present condition of the grounds and to the way in which they were used." Five months later the police were asked to keep a closer watch on the property.

Some of the earlier vigour had perhaps departed, through the removals of some of the pioneers to other areas or to The Ascension. It is worth comparing the two churches' magazines. That from The Ascension admitted to being more of a newsletter; smaller than *St Olave's News*, it was distributed free to all houses in the district, whereas the older publication was sold in declining numbers to subscribers. Articles on serious matters in *St Olave's News* tended to be wordy and worthy, and not attractive to the eye, but those in *The Ascension Church News* were much more direct. Fr Haslam dealt with confirmation in long paragraphs, not without sharp language, but Fr Sibellas used short paragraphs in catechism style to deal with questions that he thought people wanted answered. The whole tone of the newer publication was more informal; there were even jokes. For fundraising, the new District did indeed have a fair, but it also invented new schemes, such as the Million Farthing[a] Fund to make use of the least valuable coin in people's change.

After 1935 numbers started to level off and further financial burdens were placed on the parish just at the time when a future of consolidation could have been expected. Inside the church, arguments about the use of incense and about the statue of the Blessed Virgin Mary had ended, at least in public, but one suspects that they were not all truly over. Incense, at least, seems to have been introduced regardless of any remaining opposition. Fr Haslam carried many people with him, but, as Thornvale wrote, perhaps with polite understatement, he "has very definite views concerning the management of church work in the parish, and it must be confessed that those views have not always gone unchallenged."

Did St Olave's become the "Anglo-Catholic centre" that the *News* once foresaw? Fr Haslam's successor moved the services and furnishings in a more explicitly Western Rite direction, but until then it was never a convinced Red church in Canon Gunstone's spectrum, nor, I think, did anyone in the earlier days wish it to be. Deaconess Edith Todhunter wrote, soon after the new church was consecrated, that "from the start the teaching has been Anglo-Catholic, but strictly in accordance with the teaching of our Prayer Book." Thus there is reservation, but not Benediction; confession is recommended, but not held to be obligatory. Nevertheless, by 1936 the church, building and worship, could not to a casual visitor be other than Anglo-Catholic; it was certainly different from any other Anglican church in the vicinity, apart from its daughter in Pollards Hill.

---

a) At a quarter of one penny, a farthing might buy a child a small bag of sweets.

St Olave's, though High, nevertheless remained a parish where Mass was for many people a service that they attended but in which they did not fully participate, either because they were not confirmed and did not wish to be, or because they did not (understandably, we might now feel) wish to adopt the discipline of fasting communion. Fr Haddelsey identified the regularly large number of non-communicants at the main Sunday service as a defect; indeed, the criticism was made nationally in the 1930s. At Harvest Festivals, services that were established in minds as part of the Anglican year, large congregations were reported. Evening Prayer was, from early days, meant to be congregational and as simple as possible, except on festivals, and the large attendances, even allowing for the number of people who did indeed go to church twice on Sundays, may imply that some churchgoers just did not like the Mass and preferred a formal service of the Word. An older national-church Anglicanism may have survived alongside the Anglo-Catholicism of the Vicar and his supporters, with reception of Holy Communion only on great festivals.

It is far too easy to offer analysis and interpretation as if a part of the Church of God, the Body of Christ, were simply a commercial venture; we cannot possibly know how many souls were saved and lives illuminated through word, sacrament and music in the mission church and in the Byzantine spaces of A. C. Martin's building. Did those who left the area continue in the faith? Did young men called to war service carry with them the sounds of worship from their days as boys in the choir?

As I neared the end of this study of a 1930s parish, the Bible Reading Fellowship *Guidelines* was offering reflections on success. One was based on the meeting of Philip and the Ethiopian eunuch in *Acts* 8: 26–40. Philip expounded scripture and baptised, but had no news of the long-term outcome of his efforts. Paths met and diverged, leaving the Holy Spirit to do as it wished. We can but thank God for the efforts of those early parishioners and their leaders and pray for the repose of their souls.

APPENDIX A: ST OLAVE, SOUTHWARK

The first foundation of a church on the Southwark site, near the southern end of the first London Bridge(s), is presumed to date from the fifty or so years before the Norman Conquest, since the dedication is to a Scandinavian seafarer and martyr, and by 1088 a church of St Olaf in Southwark had been handed to the care of Lewes Priory by the first Earl of Surrey.[1] A church certainly existed there in 1205 and it developed into one with a layout of four aisles or longitudinal divisions. After the dissolution in 1538 of the priory at Lewes the building became a parish church.

In February 1737 damage was discovered to one of the piers on the north side. When repairs were begun, a crack developed and the north side, walls and roof collapsed. Parliament agreed to the rebuilding of the church, and Henry Flitcroft was appointed architect. The new church opened on Sunday, 6 April 1740, when Dr Herring, Bishop of Bangor, preached.[2]

After just over a century of existence the church was burnt out in a huge fire that spread from nearby Topping's Wharf in the early hours of Saturday, 19 August 1843. Selling the site and building a new church elsewhere was considered, but the costs and legal delays involved in so doing led the authorities during 1844 to use the insurance income for a restoration that included the organ, clock, furniture and fittings. Only two new bells were cast, because the tower was no longer strong enough to support a full peal, and a new clock was installed above the bell chamber. The new organ was much more than a replacement for the old; Dr Henry Gauntlett,[a] the organist, was a pioneer of a new type of pipe organ based on German models, more powerful and with a full range of pedal pipes. Archdeacon Wilberforce preached at the first service in the new building, on 17 November 1844.[3]

Less than sixty years later the Sunday congregation typically ran to five adults and about twenty charity-school children. Dwellings had been removed and replaced by wharves, offices, warehouses and railway arches. The Rector lived in Lewisham, since his rectory was unfit for habitation and was let for offices. Articles about the church appeared in *The Times* in 1907 and 1908, and in 1909 the Bishop of Southwark, Hubert Murray Burge, wrote that it was of "the greatest possible importance to wind up St Olave's as a parish and to apply its revenues to the benefit of the Church."[4]

In 1918 he promoted a Bill to amalgamate the parish of St Olave with that of nearby St John, Horsleydown, and to sell the church and churchyard site in order to provide an endowment for "an entirely new parish in a populous part of the Diocese of Southwark". The House

---

a) He is now most widely known for his hymn tune *Irby*, sung at Christmas to "Once in Royal David's City".

of Lords insisted that half of the site should become a public open space, in compliance the Disused Burial Grounds Act 1884, which thereby halved the potential sale value.

The Bill received the Royal Assent on 8 August: the tower would remain, the rest of the church would be demolished, and the western part of the resulting area of the church and churchyard would become an open space, St Olave's Gardens, fronting the river and reached through the tower. This land was to be vested in the Borough of Bermondsey for use as a public open space. The Royal Institute of British Architects compared the proposed selling and demolition of Flitcroft's "gem" with the barbarism shown by Germany in destroying French cathedrals. *The Builder* praised the church's "beautiful brick and stone front open to the river, and fine front of Portland Stone to Tooley-street".[5]

The church closed on 25 July 1919.[6] Afterwards the church building remained, its windows boarded up, and the great organ suffered piecemeal destruction; by 1924 much of the metal pipework had been taken by thieves. Recorded by several photographers,[7] the church building, except the tower, was eventually demolished in July 1926. The human remains in the churchyard went to Brookwood Cemetery[b] for reburial.

Trustees were appointed to raise money from the sale of the rectory and the eastern half of the site to pay for a new church and parsonage, wherever it might be, in the Diocese of Southwark, and to provide an endowment to help to pay for the priest of the new church. The Trustees sold the rectory in St Thomas's Street for £3,600 without much difficulty, but the slice left to them of the church site could only be sold at a price much lower than that of earlier valuations: not until 24 February 1927 was the eastern half of the land finally conveyed to the Hay's Wharf Company for £10,000.[8]

When Bermondsey Borough Council looked again at what it had gained, it was not impressed; the 'window' on the river was too small to be valuable as an open space, as indeed had been pointed out at the time. Rather than spend anything on the site, the Council promoted a Bill in Parliament to permit the sale of the tower and remaining land, which it had received free of charge after the 1918 Act, for the purpose of financing a children's playground at Tanner Street. Hay's Wharf paid £10,000 for the second slice of the St Olave's site, from which the Borough Council received £5,000[9] from selling land it was given to hold in trust.

The tower came to its end during July–August 1928, though the stump lingered till February 1930;[10] the bells were saved for re-use, and

b) The memorial at Brookwood wrongly records the demolition dates as 1923–26.

the octagonal lantern that once topped the tower can be seen today in the Tanner Street recreation ground, the space partly financed from the sale.[c] The Trustees were able, after deduction of expenses, including the cost of reburials, to transfer £7,800 in February 1930 to the Twenty-five Churches Fund,[11] and thereby to make a substantial contribution to a new church, St Olave, Mitcham.

Olaf and the church that bore his name are recalled on the corners of St Olaf House, an outstanding building from 1929–31 in Art Deco or Modernist style by H. S. Goodhart-Rendel that filled the whole St Olave's site and still catches the eye from across the river or from the rather different Tooley Street of today. Almost certainly better than anything that would have been built ten years earlier, it is the great unintended consequence in Southwark of the 1918 Act.[d]

Sources and Notes:

Unless otherwise specified, information about St Olave, Southwark, is from *PC283 St O*, Bird & Riley, C. A. Part, *Notes on the History,* D. E. Hubbard, *St. Olave's Southwark,* [all in Southwark LS], and from *Hansard*.

There are many photographs, engravings and watercolours of the Southwark churches: SC/PHL/02/1167 at LMA; in Southwark LS; online in the City of London's *Collage* collection. *The Builder*, 18/05/1844 and 25/05/1844, has a detailed architectural description of the Flitcroft church and several drawings.

1. Hubbard details the sources.
2. *London Daily Post and General Advertiser,* 08/04/1740.
3. *The Examiner,* 23/11/1844.
4. *EC* 47190/1.
5. *The Times; The Builder,* 12/07/18.
6. Order from Bishop in DS/CT/02/019 at LMA.
7. Southwark LS and LMA, SC/PHL/02/1167.
8. Land Registry, TGL 247402; LMA, DS/CT/02/019.
9. *Southwark and Bermondsey Recorder,* 11/05/28.
10. *Southwark and Bermondsey Recorder,* 14/02/30.
11. *Trustees.*

---

c) Modern photograph at www.geograph.org.uk/photo/1410297. It was made into a drinking fountain, with a plaque that recorded with inaccurate dates its origin (PB1413 and PB19443 in Southwark LS). The flagstaff with Royal crown was to be given to St George, Southwark, but what actually happened to it is not clear.

d) "An important landmark in the introduction of the Continental Modern Style into England in the 'Thirties", according to *Listed Buildings in Southwark* in Southwark LS. The building is described in some detail in Williamson and Pevsner, *London Docklands* (London 1998), and is shown on several websites (it is now part of a private hospital).

APPENDIX B: THE SOUTHWARK BEQUEST

As is well known, the Mitcham church received several items, large and small, from the church of St Olave, Southwark. However, there has been some confusion about the status of some of these gifts, especially the pulpit and one of the bells.

The small items cause no problem: they are mostly inscribed with dates and survived the 1843 fire through being kept, along with the registers, in an iron repository that was rescued by one of the churchwardens. They are:

> a silver-gilt flagon, "St Oliues Southwarke 1688"
> a silver-gilt communion cup, "S. Olaues Southwork 1630"
> a large silver-gilt plate, "St Oliues, Southwarke 1688"
> two pewter almsdishes, "St Olaves 1757 Southwark"
> two pewter almsdishes, "St Ollives Cch 1718".

No illustration of the Flitcroft interior shows the location of the font, but post-fire it was at the West end in the centre aisle. According to one report the "modern and uninteresting" font, survived the fire uninjured;[1] this runs against the impression of a composite item that most observers now gain. A "marble font with a wooden cover" appears in an inventory of 1717,[2] and the octagonal marble bowl of the present font, now cracked (from fire damage?), is fairly certainly the one seen in an 1825 illustration.[3] However, the carved pedestal seen in the same illustration is certainly not what we have now. The present plain, square base is a post-1825 (probably post-1843) addition, and the font cover, of wood, is unlikely to be a survivor of the fire.

According to a description of 1708 the pulpit was "carved, being done *Anno* 1652".[4] No pulpit is mentioned in the 1717 inventory. For the Flitcroft church a new pulpit[e] was commissioned from a Mr Pultney, complete with tester (removed *c.*1825).[5] Pictorial evidence both before and after the 1843 fire consistently shows a hexagonal pulpit of tulip shape with inlaid designs that match those on the present one; the cracks just visible in a 1918 photograph have widened since the removal to Mitcham. *Collage* 25943 shows the pulpit pre-1826, with tester, and supported on a single pillar, and this structural arrangement persisted after the fire, as can be seen in one of Sturdee's photographs.[6] Wash drawings of 1826 and 1834[7] show the pulpit and its "geometrical winding staircase"; such a staircase employs curving or continuous

---

e) E. and W. Young in *Old London Churches* (London 1956) claim that "the pulpit was a central three-decker from the start" but cite no evidence. The *Collage* picture 25943 suggests otherwise, and in the rebuilding the reading and clerk's desks were lowered, without any mention of the pulpit,[19] which suggests that they were not part of the pulpit structure.

handrails uninterrupted by newel posts, and for use at Mitcham the staircase had to be shortened to match the lower height of the pulpit on its new plinth.

It has been supposed that the pulpit escaped destruction in 1843; Sturdee's photograph of *c.*1926 is captioned "the only wooden structure that escaped the fire of 1834 [*sic*]".[8] *The Builder*, though, describing the pre-fire church, used a simple past tense: "The pulpit was a very elegant piece of design, very beautifully executed in very beautiful materials, and was, like most of the pulpits in the city of London, replete with symbolical carving and marquetry."[9]

Accounts of the fire emphasise the "total destruction" caused: "roofless"; "a few blackened timbers ... which have not fallen to ashes"; "astounding conflagration"; "ceiling in ruins"; "intense body of fire"; "blazing church". The published paintings and drawings of the fire,[10] even after allowance is made for any artistic heightening in the cause of 'sublime' effect, show the destroyed roof and the light of flames in all the window openings; a drawing made after the fire,[11] looking towards the West or tower end shows an interior with no pews and a floor strewn with broken masonry. Even though the fire was fiercest at the West end, furthest from the pulpit, it is hard to see how the pulpit could have survived unharmed when so much else in the nave was burnt or broken, although one wooden item, a sword-rest of 1674, did survive and can be seen today in Southwark Cathedral. Conclusively, though, the surveyor, Mr Allen, reported to a meeting of parishioners that "the pews to the nave, which are of wainscot with sunk and projecting panels, are for the most part crushed and ruined, as is also the reading desk and the beautifully inlaid and enriched octagon [*sic*] pulpit with its geometrical winding staircase."[12] It is true that he talks of crushing and ruin, rather than burning, but the items mentioned sound well beyond repair.

So, how old is the pulpit now at Mitcham? It shows no sign of scorching, and the documentary evidence now available seems to make clear that the pulpit in the Flitcroft church was damaged beyond repair in the 1843 fire, so it may be that a copy was made and installed in the post-fire church. There is a parallel at St Mary-at-Hill in the City of London, where much replacement carving and woodwork was done after a fire in the 1840s by W. Gibbs Rogers, done so well that, according to Sir John Betjeman, it was hard to distinguish the original work from the nineteenth-century work.[f]

The tester, or sounding-board over the pulpit, deemed surplus to requirements by 1826,[1] was made into a table and then kept in the

---

f) Unfortunately, that interior was ruined by another fire in 1988. However, there is a picture in Betjeman, *The City of London Churches* (London, Pitkin Guides, 1967) of the pulpit and a fine geometrical staircase by Rogers.

Vestry Room at Southwark. Inscribed "J. D. Jackson 1825",[13] it was "of oak, inlaid with rays emanating from a centre, in which is contained the triangle, as an emblem of the Trinity; the edge is ornamented with a carved scroll moulding; and the entire table is supported on a pillar and feet."[14] This table came to Mitcham, but is no longer extant.

In the fire the church's "fine peal of eight bells"[15] was destroyed; such was the damage to the tower that the architect would only consent to the installation of two bells. Of these two, the tenor bell, weighing just under a ton, came to Mitcham. It is inscribed "C & G MEARS FOUNDERS LONDON ST OLAVE SOUTHWARK 1844". The second bell, of about four hundredweight, was sold to Messrs Mears and Stainbank to defray costs. Mitcham also received a third bell,[g] inscribed "MR NICHOLAS FLOWER CHURCHWARDEN 1719". This date has caused some puzzlement because of the apparent evidence that the peal of bells was destroyed in 1843.

Nicholas Flower was certainly a Churchwarden of St Olave's in October 1719, when the existing six bells were taken down and recast, and two new ones added; he signed, as a witness, the memorandum submitted by Richard Phelps, the bellfounder.[16] On the Tuesday after the fire in 1843 the Surveyor reported that the flames had set light to the timber framing that had supported the peal of eight bells, "the whole of which, with the church clock, are destroyed." However, the same newspaper report made plain both that one of the bells, inscribed "R. Phelps ... 1719" remained "quite sound" and that there survived on the top of the tower a good-sized bell[h] which communicated with the clock;[17] it can be seen in a drawing made on the night of the fire.[18] The smallest of the three bells to be handed over by the Trustees was called the "clock bell" in an early church magazine; only two new ones were cast for the post-fire church, so the third, dated 1719, was probably the one from the top of the burnt-out tower, the one which survived in sound condition.

This bell was to be hung as a sanctuary bell inside the Mitcham building, but presumably practical considerations led to its being suspended from a bracket outside the tower; though the smaller bell, it nevertheless weighed 2¼ hundredweight, or 18 stones [about 113 kilograms]. The tenor bell, weighing nearly a ton [about one metric tonne], hangs from a steel joist on the North side of the building, whence its sonority fills the church inside and, outside, summons the faithful and wakens the slothful.

---

g) This bell was stolen, along with a lot of lightning conductor, in February 2013.

h) "Good sized" may be a reasonable visual assessment, but 2¼ cwt is the weight of the smallest bell in a peal. Whatever the size, it is clear that there was a bell atop the tower.

Sources and Notes:

In the last ten years a lot more material has become digitally available, notably the illustrations on the City of London's *Collage* site and the indexed newspaper collections of the British Library, so that some different answers to puzzles about the gifts from St Olave, Southwark, can now be advanced.

One potentially useful source, the Vestry Minutes for 1843–5, is no longer extant in Southwark LS.

1. *ILN*, 23/09/1843.
2. Vestry Book, Southwark LS.
3. *Collage* 25942.
4. E. Hatton, *A New View of London* (London, 1708: photocopy in *PC283 St O*).
5. Vestry Book, Southwark LS, cited in Ray Ninnis, *A Note on a Little-Noted Church* (London, Merton HS, 2001).
6. Southwark LS PB1526.
7. Southwark LS PB5102 and P15504. The latter is the basis for the line drawing published in *ILN*, 23/09/1843.
8. Southwark LS PB1526.
9. *The Builder*, 1843 p. 263.
10. *ILN*, 26/08/1843; *Collage*, 7396 and 8773.
11. *The Builder*, 1843 p. 240 and *ILN*, 13/09/1843.
12. *The Morning Post*, 23/08/1843.
13. *Inventory*.
14. *ILN*, 23/09/1843; there is a picture in *Collage*.
15. Untitled cutting in *PC283 St O*.
16. Southwark LS, Vestry Book.
17. *Lloyd's Weekly London Newspaper*, 27/08/1843.
18. *ILN*, 26/08/1843.
19. *The Times*, 17/10/1844.

APPENDIX C: NORWAY TO SOUTHWARK

In 1928 Fr Haslam lost no time in telling his first parishioners about their patron saint: "The traditional account of St. Olave may be stated as follows: 'In 1014, St Olaf, acting as the ally of King Ethelred, wrested London from the Danes by breaking down London Bridge, which had been manned against him, and drove the enemy from the fortified work of Southwark. Thereafter, in grateful memory, a church was founded in his honour, overlooking the scene of the engagement. Thus the whole district bears witness to the brave deeds of Olaf, who came to London's rescue at a critical hour in her history.' " [1]

This Olaf who gave his name to St Olave's in Southwark was born Olaf Haraldson. His father was a direct descendant of a ninth-century King of Norway. In his teen years Olaf became part of a band of Viking warriors that raided and looted along the shores of the Baltic and North Seas. It is possible that Olaf came to England in 1009 as a soldier in the Viking army that captured Canterbury. Some of this army stayed in England and fought on behalf of the English King Ethelred (traditionally and misleadingly called "the Unready"), and it was probably in this king's employ that Olaf led the attack on London Bridge that established his reputation as a rescuer of London. During a stay of about four years in England Olaf became convinced that the work begun by others to make his country a Christian kingdom should be completed. During 1014–5, before or after the attack on London, Olaf reverted to plundering, along the coast of Poitou, stayed with Duke Richard II of Normandy (many Norman nobles had kin in Norway) and was probably baptised at Rouen by Archbishop Robert.

The adult Olaf Haraldson "was not tall, but middle-sized in height, although very thick, and of good strength. He had light brown hair, and a broad face, which was white and red. He had particularly fine eyes, which were beautiful and piercing, so that one was afraid to look him in the face when he was angry."[2] The "thickness" has sometimes led to the description "Olaf the Fat", though "the Stout" is more accurate, a term of manliness, not obesity.

In 1015, still only twenty years old, he returned home with around 120 followers. Parts of Norway were then occupied by Danes and Swedes, and the rest comprised over twenty 'kingdoms', ruled by bands of warriors bound together by their loyalty to a single chieftain. Before the winter, he had gained the support of five such rulers, and within a year many more had turned to support his claim to the throne.

Olaf imposed kingdom-wide laws and insisted on their enforcement without bribes or threats; at the same time he insisted on the observance of Christian practices. He brought in dozens of foreign missionaries, some from England, some from Normandy, and chose one of them, Grimkell, sometime Bishop of Selsey, to be Bishop of Nidaros, his capital city [now called Trondheim]. Christianity was already practised in parts of Norway, and, with advice from Grimkell, Olaf rooted out customs and practices which he thought contrary to Christianity and had no compunction about using force to do so.

For the next twelve years, Norway was at peace. A large meeting in 1024 endorsed a code of laws which became the basis of the Norwegian church and state. However, after a naval defeat by Danish forces, discontented Norwegian nobles supported the invasion in 1028 by King Cnut the Great of Denmark and England. Olaf went into exile in Sweden and Russia. Convinced that he should return to Norway and complete his task, in 1030 Olaf led a small force of troops that confronted a much larger force at Stiklestad, about 65 miles northeast of the capital. As Olaf's men went into battle, they encouraged one another with the cry "Forward, forward, Christ-men! cross-men! king's men!" The day was clear, but the sky darkened and the sunlight failed— a solar eclipse. Olaf died from wounds to his left leg, stomach and neck, and his body was carried secretly from the battlefield to a grave near Nidaros.

His grave quickly became a place of pilgrimage. Stories of healings from spring water there began to circulate. Bishop Grimkell ordered a chapel to be built over Olaf's grave and his body to be exhumed; the king's body had not decayed, and a sweet odour filled the air.

Grimkell declared Olaf a saint,[a] and a national cult was thereby established. The cathedral built at Nidaros contained the body in a reliquary once kept behind the high altar, but after disturbances by Lutherans in the sixteenth century the body was reburied and its location is not now known, though a bone is preserved in a reliquary in the cathedral in Oslo.

Olaf became a symbol of Norwegian unity: there was no further resistance to the Church, extensive writing in the Norse language became increasingly common and chapels, monasteries and schools were built. Norway changed from an Iron Age, chieftain society to a medieval Christian kingdom.

Called "a lawless ruffian"[3] in the 1870s and unsaintly to modern eyes,[b] Olaf is the patron saint of Scandinavia, patron saint of bishops and abbots, of tradesmen and soldiers, and his name spread from

---

a) The designation of local holy men as saints was still the prerogative of the local bishop. Miracles and the incorruption of the body might be proofs of sanctity, besides death in the cause of Christ. Olaf's status was confirmed by the Pope in 1164.

b) "A good example of a patriot who met a violent death being accorded the title of martyr. ... Dynastic and patriotic considerations greatly helped his cult." (*Oxford Dictionary of Saints*, Oxford, 1987)

Russia to Bethlehem, from the Orkneys to Cornwall. Olaf churches can be found in the British Isles where once there were Scandinavian settlements. Of the London churches St Olave, Hart Street, survives, though Samuel Pepys seems to create more interest there than does Olaf. His miracles were illustrated in the *Carrow Psalter*, written around 1250. Usually he is shown carrying a long-handled axe, an image painted on the base of the Christus Rex figure installed in 1955–6 in the Mitcham church.

Olaf's Feast Day is observed on 29 July, by tradition the anniversary of the fatal battle in 1030, although the eclipse is now known to have occurred on 30 August.

LONDON BRIDGE IS BROKEN DOWN

According to the *Saga of Olaf Haraldson* "Olaf, and the Northmen's fleet with him, rowed quite up under the bridge, laid their cables around the piles which supported it and then rowed off with all the ships as hard as they could down the stream. ... Now as the armed troops stood thick of men upon the bridge, and there were likewise many heaps of stones and other weapons upon it, the bridge gave way; and a great part of the men upon it fell into the river, and all the others fled. ... Thereafter Southwark was stormed and taken."[4]

Though the poets and chroniclers disagree about the dates of some of the military operations of this period, they all mention the action at the bridge. A recent article concluded that the attack on London Bridge in 1014 could not be proved from other sources, but that there was no reason to disbelieve the *Saga*'s account.[5] The rhyme and its associated singing-game, though, have no likely origin in a folklore memory of Olaf.[c]

James Bird concluded in his report for the London County Council that "the claims made by various writers on behalf of St. Olave's, Southwark, have been much exaggerated. ... The church directly overlooks the spot where Olaf gained great renown in London, although in all probability its dedication had no reference to that event." Fr Haslam could therefore assure his readers that "the dedication of St. Olave's, Southwark, has no necessary connection with the warlike deeds of Olaf." His figure, with cross in one hand and sword in the other, is incised on a corner of St Olaf House in Tooley Street, whilst a statue fills one of the niches in the altar screen at Southwark Cathedral, and two schools with origins in Southwark continue to bear his name.

---

c) Samuel Laing in his 1844 translation of the Olaf saga took the literal phrase "You broke down London's bridge" and recast it as "London Bridge is broken down/Gold is won and bright renown" by recollecting the rhyme "London Bridge is broken down/Falling down, falling down", first recorded in the seventeenth century.[6]

Sources and Notes:

Saga of Olaf Haraldson tr. Laing; the former Carmelite Mission website; *The Oxford Dictionary of Saints*; lecture by Revd Simon Coupland, 1995; J. R. Hagland and B. Watson in *London Archaeologist* 12 (2005); Bruce Dickens, "The Cult of S. Olave in the British Isles" in *Saga-Book of the Viking Society* XII (1937–53), Part II, (available online, and in Southwark LS); communication from Professor John Hines.

Bird & Riley is cited several times, because its examination of Olaf's reputation was the one available to Fr Haslam and to writers of the various booklets now found in Southwark LS. The *Saga of Olaf Haraldson* is available online in *The Online Medieval and Classical Library*. The *London Archaeologist* articles are also available online.

1.   *SON*, 01/28, following Bird & Riley.
2.   *Saga of Olaf Haraldson* tr. Laing 3.
3.   Quoted in W. Rendle, *Old Southwark and its People* (London 1878).
4.   *Saga of Olaf Haraldson* tr. Laing 12; quoted in Bird & Riley.
5.   Hagland and Watson.
6.   J. Clark, "London Bridge and the archaeology of a nursery rhyme" in *London Archaeologist* 9 (2002).

APPENDIX D: ARTHUR CAMPBELL MARTIN, CVO, FRIBA

Before the First World War the architect of St Olave's pursued a successful career in designing and altering large country houses,[a] and continued in domestic architecture, though on a smaller scale,[b] after the war. From 1927 he gained regular work as the consulting architect for the Duchy of Cornwall, work which he continued until 1952, and which earned him from the Crown the honour of Companion of the Victorian Order. His first tutor in architecture, E. J. May, had himself been trained by Norman Shaw, a notable builder of country houses and proponent of vernacular and Queen Anne styles, whose work can be seen in the Bedford Park estate in West London. Martin's work outside his church and domestic work includes, in London, the Islington branch of Barclay's Bank, the rebuilding of the Duchy of Cornwall head office in Buckingham Gate and the sometime hostel for theology students of the University of London in Vincent Square, Westminster.

The Theology Faculty of King's College, London, desirous that its students should be able to learn in community, launched an appeal in 1911 for the building of a hostel in Vincent Square, Westminster. Approved by both Archbishops and by the Bishops of London and Southwark, the appeal was meant to raise £25,000 by Christmas 1912. Despite donations large and small from many sources (Queen Mary donated £25), the Faculty had to agree to postpone the building of the south wing—library and chapel as well as accommodation—and of the Warden's house. Martin was appointed architect in June 1912 after approval of his preliminary sketch plans, the foundation stone was laid on 6 May 1913, and the Bishop of London declared the hostel open on 26 February 1914.

During the First World War Martin served in the Royal Fusiliers. Commissioned in January 1915, he sailed for France in November that year, only for his unit to be broken up in 1916, when he was sent to the Staff College. In January 1917 he became one of the first New Army officers to be appointed as an officer of a Company of Gentlemen Cadets at Sandhurst[c]—such posts had previously been the preserve of the

---

a) e.g. South Wraxall Manor in Wiltshire, Guisboro' Hall in Yorkshire, Outer Down, Chagford, in Devon.

b) He won a £500 prize in the *Daily Mail* Workers' Homes Competition 1919 and published *The Small House* in 1906, 1909 and again in the 1920s. His 1919 Rural Area home design is illustrated in *The Builder* 16/05/19.

c) The statement to this effect in the RIBA Obituary seems to be supported by the initials "N.A." against Martin's name and that of another subaltern to be found in the Sandhurst *Orders* for January 1917; no officer appointed in the preceding six months is so described.

career soldier—and was asked for his opinion on the prospects of rebuilding the chapel. On his own initiative he drew up plans and in January 1918 he was appointed, while still a serving Lieutenant, as the architect for the rebuilding and enlargement of the chapel at Sandhurst. Gazetted out in 1919 with the rank of Captain, he continued working on the chapel; the first part was consecrated in May 1921, but the project was not completed, through shortage of funds, until 1937.

The chapel at Sandhurst needed enlargement to accommodate the increased number of cadets, and also because there was not enough space to record on its columns the names of the officer cadets who had fallen in such numbers during the Great War. In Martin's scheme the new building was built at right angles across the earlier one, with the chancel and sanctuary on one side and the nave on the other. An unidentified "eminent architect" described this idea as "a stroke of genius". The series of semicircular arches in the aisles,[d] the barrel vaults and the dome are Byzantine features that Martin repeated and developed elsewhere; moreover, they are constructed in reinforced concrete, a material until then little used in churches.

Another war memorial appeal, at King's College, London, was set up to add the missing wing at the Vincent Square hostel "in conformity with the plans already prepared"; a coloured drawing shows a three-storey building in Gothic style, with the chapel on the top floor. Nothing immediate came from this appeal, but a fresh attempt was made in 1927, in view of the imminent celebration of King's College's centenary. The Hostel Committee decided that the chapel should now be on the ground floor, supporting the library and then two storeys of student accommodation. The Gothic style was dropped, in favour of matching the exterior to the earlier building.

Martin provided groined vaulting in concrete for the chapel roof, supported by reinforced concrete piers, and Truscon joists supported the upper floors.[e] The chapel, only fifteen feet high, was rectangular, with a semicircular, domed apse. The three bays could accommodate about a hundred people. *The Builder* noted "groined vaulting in concrete springing from green marble columns with well-carved capitals" in the otherwise "plain Byzantine interior". Building began in April 1928, and the Archbishop of Canterbury dedicated the chapel on 26 June 1929. The former hostel is now the Grange Wellington Hotel, 71 Vincent Square. The chapel, plainly decorated, was a meeting room for

---

d) Similar arches appeared even in his houses: see Lees, p. 43.

e) The Trussed Concrete Steel Company had provided reinforcement for Martin's 1913 building and for the vaulting at Sandhurst, and was employed by Martin at Mitcham.

conferences, but at the time of writing the hotel is undergoing refurbishment.

Martin's churches are three in number: St Olave, Mitcham, built 1930–31, St Luke, Milber, on the outskirts of Newton Abbot, begun in the 1930s but not completed until 1963, and St Luke, Camberwell, designed in 1953 and completed after his retirement. They all have Byzantine features, and the church in Milber has a remarkable ground plan of three diverging naves, a shape dreamt by Revd Keble Martin, the architect's younger brother, who was the parish priest.

There might have been a fourth church: when Fr Haslam later in his ministry found himself in the parish of St Mark, Surbiton, Martin was asked to provide plans for a new church to be built on the footprint of the one destroyed by bombing in October 1940. The plans show a fairly dull scheme in brick Gothic style, similar in appearance to the original (as was locally expected); inside, all the seating allowed a view of chancel and altar—an improvement. Because of post-war shortages nothing was built, and in 1954–5 a different architect was commissioned to build the church. Martin's church reputation lives through the three more adventurous buildings, designed to use modern materials in a practical and uncluttered historic style.

Martin was born at Radley College to parents with relations in public schools, law, banking and the Church of England; he was educated at Winchester College. In adult life he took a serious interest in Church affairs: he was a member of the House of Laity in the Church Assembly and, at a local level, was a Churchwarden at St Jude, Englefield Green, near Egham, whose vicarage he designed. Happily married for over fifty years, he was a man of distinction in character as well as in professional skill: two of his assistants worked with him for thirty years and wrote of his "placid, happy nature", and the Land Steward of the Duchy remembered his courtesy, dry sense of humour and love of wildlife.

Sources:

RIBA Journal, 70 (October 1963), p. 421; some dates corrected.
Stocker.
Lees.
Blackburne & Waring.
Who's Who in Architecture, 1914, 1926.
St Jude's, Englefield Green, parish website.
WO/374/46344 in The National Archives.
King's College, London, Archives, KAS/AD2/F66 & 67; KAS/AD4/F15 & 19;
KAC/M17 & 19; K PLANS 4.
Royal Military Academy Sandhurst, Archives, HIST: Specification and Estimate;
Royal Military Academy Sandhurst, Archives, Orders 1916–7.
The Builder, 24/01/30.
Surrey LS, 2217/5/4 a, b, c.
Surrey Comet, 15/03/47.

www.royalmemorialchapel.com and Lees have pictures and a plan of the Sandhurst chapel.

APPENDIX E: THE ORGAN

There is no clear evidence of what instrument was used at first to accompany services in the mission church, but in July 1928 a restored two-manual reed organ, described as the "1860 hand-blown American organ, with small pedal board" from the Deaconess Institute in Clapham was offered to the church. However, by the end of the year a second-hand Broadwood grand piano had been bought for £20. By May 1930 this had replaced the reed organ, which was soon sold for £5, the proceeds being used to purchase choir music.

The 1931 pipe organ was supplied for £870, inclusive of console and blower, by Rest Cartwright and Son;[a] it had been first built at a pre-1914 cost of around £2,000.[1] Fr Haslam wrote, for a restoration appeal in 1958, that the organ "belonged to one of the Barclay family (bankers) and was kept in a mansion in Essex." The *National Pipe Organ Register*, though, has it as a former chamber organ by T. C. Lewis, and the crest on the case as the Courage arms.[2]

The crest on the case is in fact one granted in 1738 to Mary Goodhugh of Kent: the arms were to be borne by herself and by the heirs of her body, but she died childless.[3] The motto *Audax atque fidelis* is not in any standard reference work.

The Courage/Lewis claim can probably be rejected, for the "mansion in Essex" was undoubtedly Monkhams at Woodford, Essex, owned from 1864 until his death by Henry Ford Barclay. Arnold Hills bought the house and estate at auction in July 1892 and had an organ placed at the top of the hall stairs.[4] A photograph[5] taken by him on 14 December 1893 shows the present case, complete with coat of arms and motto, before being truncated to sit on the shelf of the church organ chamber. The surname Hills is that of Mary Goodhugh's brother, Richard Hills, though a lineal connection has yet to be established, as has the origin of the motto. The builder's identity is as yet unknown; Rest Cartwright did not start his career until the new century had begun. At the time of printing [2013], research continues.

Notes:

1. *Minutes*, 07/11/30.
2. *NPOR*, N13820.
3. Communication from Mr Timothy Duke [Chester Herald].
4. *Essex Review*, 14 (1905) p. 163.
5. English Heritage Archive, BL12543.

---

a) This London firm was founded by Rest Cartwright (1864–1945) and went through several changes of legal title. Bought out by Ivor Davies c.1938, the company was wound up in 1972. (*NPOR* and *London Gazette*)

1931

Great

Open diapason	8ft
Gt diapason and clarabella	8ft
Dulciana	8ft
Clarinet	8ft
Principal	4ft
Wald flöte	4ft

Swell

Double diapason	16ft
Lieblich gedackt	8ft
Salicional	8ft
Oboe	8ft
Voix célestes	8ft
Gemshorn	4ft
Piccolo	2ft

Tremulant

Balanced swell pedal

Pedal

Bourdon	16ft
Lieblich bourdon	16ft
Bass flute	8ft

Couplers

Swell to Great
Swell to Pedal
Great to Pedal

6 pistons on manuals

Range: manuals CC to a^2
       pedals CCC to F

Action: part pneumatic, part mechanical

Spellings: 1931 from *Musical Opinion*, March 1931; 1961 from stop tabs of present console.

1961

Great

Lieblich bourdon	16ft
Open diapason	8ft
Claribel	8ft
Dulciana	8ft
Clarinet	8ft
Principal	4ft
Waldflute	4ft
Fifteenth	2ft

Swell

Lieblich gedakt	8ft
Salicional	8ft
Oboe	8ft
Voix celeste	8ft
Gemshorn	4ft
Twelfth	2 2/3
Piccolo	2ft

Tremulant

Balanced swell pedal

Pedal

Sub bass	32ft
Bourdon	16ft
Lieblich bourdon	16ft
Bass flute	8ft
Octave flute	4ft

Couplers

Swell to Great
Swell to Pedal
Great to Pedal
Swell octave
Swell sub-octave
6 pistons on manuals
4 pedal pistons

Range: manuals CC to a^2
       pedals CCC to F

Action: electro-pneumatic

New console in 1961

Pitch: A = 450 cps

APPENDIX F: CHURCH CHOIRS

Fr Haslam could recruit his choir because of the assumption that most self-respecting Anglican churches, except small or remote ones, had boys in the choir. Certainly churches that had Anglo-Catholic leanings, even mild ones, had robed male choirs placed, almost always, in inward-facing choir stalls in the chancel, between the altar and the nave. Low or very small churches might have women in the choir,[1] whilst the days of instrumentalists or charity children in a gallery were long gone. By 1927 the Anglican choral sound could be heard on the wireless in broadcasts of Choral Evensong, and Ernest Lough's best-selling record of "Oh, for the wings of a dove" defined the English boy treble's voice. For Fr Haslam, though, a boys' choir reached beyond music to the formation of Christian character, so that the first off-site youth activity at St Olave's was a choir camp; the Boy Scouts came later.

The establishment of robed choirs in the Church of England developed alongside the Oxford and Cambridge Movements in doctrine and church-building: the emphasis on the Eucharist as the main service of the Church made the altar at the East end of the chancel a point of focus that required, in more 'advanced' churches, robed assistants. At Leeds Parish Church the new building (1839–41) provided ample accommodation in the chancel for the robed choir there, one that set new standards in the rendering of the musical parts of formal worship. This cathedral-like ideal became the model in thousands of churches,[2] as a part of the pursuit of dignity and order that was an unstoppable force in the Victorian church.[3]

Dr John Jebb, a pioneer campaigner for cathedral-model choirs in chancels, wrote colourfully in 1845 that, with its "white-robed companies of men and boys, stationed at each side of her chancels", the Church of England had "made the nearest possible approach to a primitive and heavenly pattern".[4] These choristers became for about a century an expected part of church services in England, though even by 1961 Dom Anselm Hughes could reflect on the "disappearance of the boy choirs in numerous places".[5]

Boy singers maintained their contribution to public worship at St Olave's until the 1970s. The choir organisations before the outbreak of war provided Christian, as well as musical, teaching, opportunities for leadership and the experience of social and outdoor life beyond the parental home. Fr Haslam set great value on the summer camps: "Camp is a very great opportunity of getting to know each other better, and we can never forget those happy days when we were enabled to work, play and pray together. ... It is a wonderful means of developing and bringing out all that is best in their character."[6]

It has become easy for the present age to sneer at all this, or to condemn its provision only for boys, but some, at least, of those boys so favoured grew into the churchmen of the next generation, whereas in the age of equality men make up less than forty per cent of congregations.[7]

Notes:

1.   Stephenson, p. 32.
2.   Kenneth R. Long, *The Music of the English Church* (London, 1972), p. 329.
3.   See Chadwick 1966, pp. 517–9.
4.   Quoted in Anson, p. 73.
5.   Hughes, p. 131.
6.   *SON* 09/28, 09/32. See also Gunson pp. 191, 290.
7.   See Christopher Ducker's thesis at www.theduckers.org/media/disbanded brothers.

APPENDIX G: THE SUPPORTING CAST

CLERGY

Davis, Vincent Paul, 1906–1989: Curate 1931–4; Residence: 46 Beckway Road. Diocese of Queenstown (SA) 1934–8; Vicar, St Mary, Ewell, 1944–68; Rector of Stainby (Lincs.) 1968–73.

Trapp, Eric Joseph 1910–1993: Curate 1934–7; Residence: 396 Northborough Road. Basutoland and Orange Free State 1937–47; Bishop of Zululand 1947–57; Secretary of SPG/USPG from 1957; Bishop of Bermuda 1970–5. "Exceptional ability as a preacher". (*Advertiser*, 07/01/37)

Harrison, Roger Montague 1908–1980: Curate 1937–40; Residence: 44 St Olave's Walk. Married. Vicar, St Peter, Southampton, 1944–54; St Ambrose, Bournemouth, from 1954. "Never upset ... a serene and tranquil mind". (*SON* 03/40)

Sibellas, Leonard Goby 1904–1958: Curate, and Priest-in-Charge of the Church of The Ascension. Parishes in Yorkshire from 1940; Vicar of Cantley from 1953.

DEACONESSES

Todhunter, Edith 1873–1957: Deaconess February 1928–September 1930. Residence: 4 Long Thornton Road. At St Barnabas, Southfields, in 1936–7.

Trotter, Kate: Deaconess 1936–June 1938. Residence: 46 Beckway Road. At St Bartholomew, Camberwell, in 1929–30. A "most assiduous visitor". (*Minutes*, APCM, 1937)

CHURCHWARDENS

Pailthorpe, Frederick Gerald, 1892–1958: M.B., Ch.B. Liverpool 1921, L.R.C.P., L.R.C.S. Edinburgh, L.R.F.P.S. Glasgow 1917, Temporary Surgeon R.N. Lay Reader from 1932.

Rudolph, Harry, 1882–1950: carpenter.

VERGER

Carey, William John: 1879–1940: sometime Dragoon Guard.

TABLES

TABLE A

Population of Mitcham and Croydon, 1931

Age distribution per thousand men:

Ages	0–4	5–19	20–39	40+
Mitcham	91	253	373	283
Croydon	75	248	323	354

Average ages by gender:

	Male	Female
Mitcham	29.5	30.8
Croydon	32.3	34.4

TABLE B

Church of England National Statistics 1928–39

(a) Baptisms (b) Confirmations* (c) Sunday Schools (in 1000s)
(d) Easter Communions (e) Electoral Rolls

	(a)	(b)	(c)	(d)	(e)
1928	437,769	200,838	1,829	2,339,283	3,641,536
1939	388,942	157,627	1,434	2,245,102	3,390,125
Change %	– 11	– 22	– 22	– 4	– 7

* Confirmations in Southwark Diocese were: 10,123 in 1929 and 8,689 in 1938 (– 14%).

Sources: Table A: 1931 Census, Surrey. Table B: *SDD*; Currie et al., *Churches and Churchgoers* (London, 1977).

TABLE C

1. Regular giving schemes, 1931 and 2010:

	1931		2010
Members	180		42
Total given in year	£398		£13,495
at 2010 value	*£21,100*		*£13,495*
Total per member	£2. 4s. 0d.		£321
at 2010 value	*£117*		*£321*

2. Loose collections, 1934 and 2010:

	1934		2010
	£80		£1,045
at 2010 value	*£4,430*		*£1,045*

TABLE D

Expenditure on (a) staff and Quota; (b) mission

	1934	1938	2010
Staff + Quota	£167	£293	£21,379
at 2010 value	*£9,250*	*£14,600*	*£21,379*
Mission and Charity	£62	£43	£1,944
at 2010 value	*£3,430*	*£2,140*	*£1,944*

Staff and Quota: pre-war payments are for curates and (1938) Deaconess; Organist and Verger; Quota. 2010 payments are for Vicar's expenses, organists, hall caretaker, Fairer Shares [Quota].

Sources: parish magazines; 2010 parish accounts; www.MeasuringWorth.com (Retail Price Index).

ENDNOTES

Much of the narrative is constructed from church magazines (*SON*), Church Council and Annual Meeting records (*Minutes*), and from local newspapers. Both *The Mitcham Advertiser and Surrey County Reporter* and the *Balham, Tooting, Mitcham News & Mercury* had pseudonymous correspondents, Thornvale and Thornsome, based in Long Thornton. References from all these sources are supplied only occasionally.

Chapter 1

For more about Lonesome and Long Thornton, see Montague.

1. Article produced by St Andrew's parish, Wandsworth LS.
2. *News*, 13/03/31.
3. Constance Pope, *Around Manor Road, Mitcham* (London, Merton HS, 1989).
4. *Advertiser*, 12/04/28.
5. Letter from publicity agent of the Ratepayers' Association, *News*, 21/09/28.
6. *Red Book of Commerce* 1929; *Kelly's Directory of the Chemical Industries* 1930.
7. Isaac.
8. Comment from John W. Brown about his father.
9. *Daily Mirror*, 28/11/13; Isaac.
10. *UDC*, 08/04/24.

Chapter 2

Information on the Fund and other Southwark churches from Richardson.

1. For Bishop Garbett, see Smyth and *ODNB*.
2. Richardson; Garbett 1944, p. 27.
3. *UDC*.

Chapter 3

Information about other Southwark churches from Richardson.

1. Publicity Agent of Residents' Association in *News*, 21/09/28.
2. Land Registry documents.
3. LMA, DS/F/1094.
4. *SDG*, 03/28.
5. Recollection of the late Mrs Joan Bartlett.
6. Amy Watkinson, *The Parish of St. Olave, Mitcham* 1981, Surrey LS 2635/1/3b.
7. *SON*, 06/76.
8. Richardson.

Chapter 4

Chapter heading: comment by Fr Davis, the first curate, in *SON*, 04/81.

1. Smyth, pp. 155, 167.
2. *Wimbledon Herald*, 15/02/08. The Sutton curacies do not appear in *Crockford*.
3. *Sutton Directory*, 1896, in Sutton LS.
4. Christ Church magazines in Sutton LS.

5. *Wimbledon Herald*, 21/02/08; *Sutton Advertiser*, 21/02/08; *Inquests, Southwark 1901–1932*, LMA.
6. Information from *The Eagle* and college records kindly supplied by the Biographical Librarian of St John's College, Cambridge.
7. Pickering, pp. 106–117.
8. The National Archives, WO374/31809.
9. St Anne, Wandsworth, church magazines, 1921 (LMA).
10. Clarke, p. 253; *Lost Churches* on Diocese of Southwark website.
11. *Visitation 1936*.
12. Letter from Fr Paul Davis in *SON*, 04/81.
13. *Crockford*.
14. Sometime parish website of St Mark, Surbiton, quoting a pamphlet *Surbiton Parish Church: Beauty for Ashes* (1960).
15. *Surrey Comet*, 09/10/54.
16. Surrey LS, 2217/5/113.
17. *Surrey Comet*, 15/03/47. The drawings are in Surrey LS, 2217/5/4 a, b, c.
18. *Surrey Comet*, 27/11/54.
19. Garbett 1944, p. 14.
20. Gunstone, p. 132.

Chapter 5

1. Garbett 1955, p. 51.
2. Charles Wesley, "Love Divine".
3. Service Registers, Surrey LS, 2051/1/15, 2051/1/16.
4. Hebert.

Chapter 6

1. *Hansard,* 2637, 15/12/27.
2. Sir William Joynson-Hicks, *Hansard*, 2550, 15/12/27.
3. "Enabling Act" in *ODCC*.
4. From a Commission of Inquiry in 1919; quoted in David L. Edwards, *Christian England*, iii (London, 1984), p. 361.
5. Quoted in Maiden, p. 101.
6. Maiden p. 41.
7. Bishop William Temple in *Evening Standard*, 08/02/27.
8. Sir William Joynson-Hicks, *Hansard* 2545, 15/12/27.
9. *Daily Chronicle*, 17/12/27.
10. Commander Kenworthy M.P. in *Daily Express*, 16/12/27.
11. *Daily Express*, 17/12/27.
12. *SON*, 02/28 and *SDG*, 02/28.
13. *SDG*, 07/28 and 09/29.
14. *Daily Mirror*, 17/12/27.
15. *Daily Express*, 08/02/27.
16. Comments from *News*, 12/12/30 and 19/12/30 (my italics).
17. Fr Marcus Atlay, quoted in Gunstone, p. 344.
18. Smyth, p. 195; quoted with comments in Hughes, pp. 91–2.
19. From Gunstone.

Chapter 7

The disputes over the change of organist and over ritual are covered in detail in *News* 12/12/30, 19/12/30, 09/01/31, 06/02/31 and 17/04/31.

1. Chadwick 1970, p. 357.

2.   Richardson, p. 93.
3.   *Sutton Advertiser*, 11/11/37.
4.   St Anne, Wandsworth, church magazine, 08/21, in LMA.
5.   *Advertiser*, 03/10/29.
6.   *The Streatham News*, 30/01/31.
7.   Pickering, pp. 126, 258.
8.   *Archbishops' Second Commission of Enquiry 1918*, quoted in Gray, p. 57.
9.   Smyth, p. 179; Correspondence of Archbishop Lang, 127 ff 218–24, Lambeth Palace Library.
10. *Advertiser*, 28/02/24.
11. Garbett 1944, p. 33.
12. *Advertiser*, 04/08/38.

Chapter 8

The *ICBS* folder for St Olave's and *EC* 91151/1 are the basis of this chapter.

1.   *London Gazette*, 08/11/29.
2.   Article by A. C. Martin in *Souvenir*.
3.   Blackburne & Waring; picture in *The Builder*, 01/26.
4.   J. F. M. Smallwood, *Southwark: some biographical information*, Lambeth Palace Library.
5.   King's College, London, Archives, KAC M19.
6.   Garbett 1944, p. 26.

Chapter 9

The account is from *News* 23/01/31, abridged, and paragraphing edited.

Chapter 10

Unless otherwise indicated, structural details come from *ICBS* and *EC* 91151/1. Martin's comments are all from his article in *Souvenir*.

1.   Hebert, p. 240.
2.   *The Guardian*, 31/03/33.
3.   *RIBA Journal*, 14/10/33.
4.   *SDG*, 03/31.
5.   Richardson, p. 88.
6.   Paul Sharrock in *Surveys* 2003.
7.   Doreen Yarwood, *Encyclopaedia of Architecture* (London, 1985).
8.   Clarke; Yelton & Salmon.
9.   List of contractors in *Souvenir*.
10. Ray Gosney in *Surveys* 1998.
11. Advertisement in *Souvenir*.
12. *EC* 91834/1.
13. Letter in *The Guardian*, 01/08/30.
14. Letter from D. James, Churchwarden, 1972, in *ICBS*.
15. Report of South London Church Fund AGM quoted in *SON*, 07/39.
16. *Souvenir*.
17. *Surveys* 2011.
18. Stocker; notes *c.*1955 in Surrey LS 2217/5/113.
19. Letter dated Easter Monday, 1955, RMC archives, HIST.

Chapter 11

1. Alan Wilkinson, *The Church of England and the First World War* (London, 1996), p. 178.
2. Garbett 1925.
3. Minutes of Mothers' Union 22/07/37, Surrey LS, 9182/3/3.
4. Communication from Fr Jeremy Paisey.
5. Gunstone, plate 16.
6. Gregory Dix, *The Shape of the Liturgy* (London, 1945), pp. 711–2; Chadwick 1970, p. 350.
7. Archbishop of York, quoted in Yelton, p. 66.

Chapter 12

1. Quoted in Gray, p. 305.
2. Quoted in Gray, p. 303.
3. Revd Neville Talbot, quoted in Gray, p. 69.
4. *Chaplains' Report 1918,* quoted in Gray, p. 64.
5. Hebert, p. 210.

Chapter 13

1. *ODCC.*

Chapter 14

1. Gunstone, pp. 34–5.
2. Recollection of the late Fr Roy Brenchley.

Chapter 15

1. *East Mitcham Log,* 10/24; article by W. Dalton in *Long Thornton Pioneer,* 07/33, Merton LS.
2. *Evening News,* 02/09/27 and 30/09/27.
3. *Visitation 1929* and *Visitation 1936.*
4. *Visitation 1929.*
5. Letters from Messrs Curtis and Cadman in *News,* 10/05/29 and 13/09/29; *Advertiser,* 07/02/29.
6. Cited by James H. Johnson in J. Coppock & H. Prince (eds.), *Greater London* (London, 1964).
7. *UDC.*
8. *Visitation 1929* and *Visitation 1936; ICBS; EC* NB/37/171 and NB/37/268.
9. *SDG,* 05/33.
10. *UDC,* 16/04/29.
11. Jackson, pp. 190–1.
12. *UDC.*
13. *Visitation 1929.*
14. Confirmation register, Surrey LS.
15. Advertisement in the *Evening News,* London, 02/09/27.

Chapter 16

1. *EC* PB 93689.
2. *SDG,* 07/36.
3. *EC* 91151 is the source for this paragraph.
4. *EC* 91151.

5.   *Ascension*, 11/35.
6.   *Advertiser*, 04/02/37.
7.   *EC Reports*, 1935.
8.   *EC* 74641.

Chapter 17

1.   Smyth, pp. 152–3.
2.   *MPC*, 08/29.
3.   *MPC*, 05/29.
4.   *News*, 12/12/30.
5.   Jackson, p. 191.
6.   MeasuringWorth.com.
7.   Agatha Chapman, *Wages and Salaries in the United Kingdom 1920–1938* (Cambridge, 1953); see also tables in Lionel Munby, *How Much is that Worth?* (Salisbury, 1996), pp. 60–3.
8.   *Advertiser*, 27/02/36; *UDC*.
9.   *Ascension*, 12/35.
10. *Advertiser*, 02/10/30.
11. Mowat, p. 456.

Chapter 18

1.   *Visitation 1929*; *Visitation 1936*.
2.   *Visitation 1936*.
3.   *Minutes*; *Visitation 1929*; *Visitation 1936*.
4.   Garbett 1916.
5.   Roger Lloyd, *The Church of England in the Twentieth Century* ii (London, 1950), pp. 63–4.
6.   A. Hastings, *A History of English Christianity, 1920–1990* (London, 1991), p. 67.
7.   *SDG*, 03/28.
8.   St Nicholas Fayre Souvenir Programme, 1938.

Chapter 19

The story is covered in *News* 12/12/30, 19/12/30, 17/04/31.

1.   *SON*, 12/61.
2.   Recollection of the late Fr Roy Brenchley.

Chapter 20

1.   St Nicholas Fayre Souvenir Programme, 1938.
2.   Letter in *Musical Times*, 12/30.
3.   Gunstone, p. 290.
4.   Munday, p. 10.

Chapter 21

1.   *News*, 21/06/35; table in Mowat, p. 464.
2.   Munday, pp. 7–8.

Chapter 22

Title: *Advertiser* 02/06/38, reporting the Bishop of Southwark at the Institution of Fr Haddelsey: "A fine tradition had been established."

1.   *New Directions*, 03/2003.
2.   *SDG*, 05/33.
3.   F. G. Curtis in *News*, 07/08/36.
4.   Munday, p. 9.
5.   *SON*, 11/50.

REFERENCES

The *Southwark Diocesan Gazette* for this period can be found inside the church magazines of many parishes. LMA: London Metropolitan Archives; LPL: Lambeth Palace Library; LS: Local Studies or County Archives; HS History/Historical Society.

Advertiser	*The Mitcham Advertiser and Surrey County Reporter*, Merton LS.
Anson	Peter F. Anson, *Fashions in Church Furnishings 1840–1940* (London, 1960).
Ascension	*The Ascension Church News*, Merton LS.
Bird & Riley	J. Bird and W. E. Riley, *Report on the Architectural History of St Olave's Southwark*, Southwark LS.
Blackburne & Waring	H. W. Blackburne and H. A. Waring, *The Chapel of the Royal Military College, Sandhurst* (Aldershot, 1922).
Chadwick 1966	Owen Chadwick, *The Victorian Church Part One* (London, 1966).
Chadwick 1970	Owen Chadwick, *The Victorian Church Part Two* (London, 1970).
Clarke	B. F. L. Clarke, *Parish Churches of London* (London, 1966).
Collage	*City of London Library & Art Gallery Electronic* (Online).
Crockford	*Crockford's Clerical Directory*.
EC	Ecclesiastical Commissioners files, Church of England Record Centre.
EC Reports	Annual Reports of the Ecclesiastical Commissioners.
Garbett 1916	C. F. Garbett, *Baptism* (London, 1916).
Garbett 1925	C. F. Garbett, *Reservation* (London, 1925).
Garbett 1944	C. F. Garbett, MS Memoirs (York Minster Library, COLL 1982 section V).
Garbett 1955	C. F. Garbett, *The Claims of the Church of England*, (2nd edn, London, 1955).
Gray	D. C. Gray, *The Evolution of the Parish Communion in the Church of England* (PhD thesis, University of Manchester, 1985, LPL H5149.C5G7.
Gunstone	John Gunstone, *Lift High the Cross* (Norwich, 2010).
Hansard	Reports of Proceedings in Parliament (online).
Hebert	A. G. Hebert, *Liturgy and Society* (London, 1935).
Hughes	Anselm Hughes, *The Rivers of the Flood* (London, 1961).
ICBS	Incorporated Church Building Society files, LPL.
ILN	*Illustrated London News*.
Inventory	St Olave's Church: MS inventory compiled in 1950.
Isaac	I. C. A. Isaac, *Vale Vistas* (London, Streatham Society, 1982).
Jackson	Alan A. Jackson, *Semi-Detached London* (London, 1973).
Lees	Hilary Lees, *So Runs My Dream: The Story of Arthur and Keble Martin* (Tiverton, 2001).
Maiden	John G. Maiden, *National Religion and the Prayer Book Controversy, 1927–1928* (Woodbridge, 2009).

Minutes	Minutes of St Olave's Church Council meetings and Annual Parish Meetings, Surrey LS.
Montague	E. N. Montague, *Pollards Hill Commonside East and Lonesome* (London, Merton HS, 2002).
Mowat	Charles Loch Mowat, *Britain between the Wars* (London, 1955).
MPC	Mitcham Parish Church Magazines (Merton LS).
Munday	Christine Munday, *The Story of the Long Thornton ... Association* (London, Merton HS, 1990).
News	*Balham, Tooting, Mitcham News & Mercury* (Merton LS).
NPOR	*The National Pipe Organ Register* (online).
ODCC	*Oxford Dictionary of the Christian Church* (Oxford, 1997).
ODNB	*Oxford Dictionary of National Biography* (Oxford, 2004 and online).
PC273 St O	*Press cuttings: St Olave, Southwark*, Southwark LS.
PC625.7	*Press cuttings: Tooley Street and Tanner Street*, Southwark LS.
Pickering	W. S. F. Pickering, *Anglo-Catholicism* (2nd edn, Cambridge, 2008).
Richardson	Kenneth Richardson, *The 'Twenty-five' Churches of the Southwark Diocese* (London, The Ecclesiological Society, 2002). (text available online).
SDD	*Southwark Diocesan Directory*, Guildhall Library.
SDG	*Southwark Diocesan Gazette.*
Smyth	Charles Smyth, *Cyril Forster Garbett, Archbishop of York* (London, 1959).
SON	*St Olave's News*, Surrey LS and Merton LS.
Souvenir	*Official Souvenir of Consecration*, St Olave's Church.
Stephenson	Colin Stephenson, *Merrily On High* (Norwich, 2008).
Stocker	Ann Stocker, in *Transactions of The Association for Studies in the Conservation of Historic Buildings,* 21 (1996), RIBA Library.
Surveys	Architects' Quinquennial Surveys (St Olave's Church).
Trustees	Trustees of Saint Olave Church Act, ledger, LMA, P71/OLA/062.
UDC	Transactions of Mitcham Urban District Council, Merton LS.
Visitation 1929	Bishop of Southwark's Visitation Book, LMA, DS/VB 10).
Visitation 1936	Bishop of Southwark's Visitation Book, LMA, DS/VB 12.
Yates	Nigel Yates, *The Oxford Movement and Anglican Ritualism* (London, The Historical Association, 1983).
Yelton	Michael Yelton, *Anglican Papalism* (London, 2005).
Yelton & Salmon	Michael Yelton and John Salmon, *Anglican Church-Building in London 1915–1945* (Reading, 2007).

INDEX